RED SCARF GIRL

RED SCARF GIRL

★★A MEMOIR OF THE★★
CULTURAL REVOLUTION

JI★LI JIANG

FOREWORD BY

DAVID HENRY HWANG

SCHOLASTIC INC.

New York   Toronto   London   Auckland   Sydney
Mexico City   New Delhi   Hong Kong

ISBN 0-439-06300-0

12 11 10 9 8 7 6 5 4 3 2 1   9/9 0 1 2 3 4/0

Printed in the U.S.A.   40

First Scholastic printing, January 1999

Typography by Steve Scott

To my dearest Grandma,
who would be so happy if she
could see this book

★★ ACKNOWLEDGMENTS ★★

I would like to thank my dear parents, who have given me their unconditional love wherever I go and whatever I do. I want to thank my brother and sister for being with me whether life is hard or easy. I also thank my friends who have believed in me and supported me, pulling and pushing me along in the process of writing this book. These include:

Florence Chun and Annie & Rick Bernstein, who have helped me grow ever since I arrived in the United States; Barbara Fishlowitz-Leong, who gave me the inspiration to start this book; Deborah Rogin and Mary Tewksbury, who frankly critiqued my work; J. W. Ellsworth, who generously provided me his legal advice; Iris Wiley and Sharon Yamamoto, editors at University of Hawaii Press, who saw the potential in my manuscript and gave me the courage to continue.

Many thanks to my agent, Kathleen Anderson, for her faith in my book, and to my editor, Ginee Seo, whose profound understanding and proficient editing brought out the essence of my story.

A thousand thanks to Vivian Xue, whose wholehearted support helped me to complete this book.

Finally, my thanks to Craig Shaw, whose constructive suggestions and meticulous refinement of the book greatly enhanced its focus and readability.

★★ CONTENTS ★★

In China people are usually called by their surnames first. Thus, in this book you will see Ji-li Jiang called Jiang Ji-li by her teachers and friends. Usage of the first name is reserved for close friends and family.

There are only one hundred surnames in Chinese, so it is not unusual for people who are not related to have the same name. Chinese women do not change their surnames when they marry, although they may sometimes be addressd by a married name as a sign of respect.

A more detailed explanation of some of the words, ideas, and people in this book may be found in the glossary at the back.

Most Chinese words written in English are pronounced as they are written, with some exceptions:

> The letter "c" when followed by a
> vowel is pronounced "ts."
> The letter "q" is pronounced "ch."
> The letter "x" is pronounced "sh."
> The letter "z" is pronounced "dz."
> The letter combination "zh" is
> pronounced "j."

★★ FOREWORD ★★

When I was a small boy, my grandmother told me about a distant uncle who was living in China during the Cultural Revolution. He promised to send a picture of himself to his relatives in America. If conditions were good, he said, he would be standing. If they were bad, he would be sitting. In the photo he sent us, my grandmother whispered, he was lying down!

As a Chinese American born in Southern California, my perception of China's Cultural Revolution was limited to stories that filtered out from the few relatives who had stayed behind. As I grew older and China opened up to the West, I learned more. A friend who went to China to teach English returned with a raft of tales from survivors, each more horrible than the last.

The seeds of the Great Proletarian Cultural Revolution had been planted many years before it burst forth in 1966. Seventeen years earlier, in 1949, the charismatic revolutionary Mao Ze-dong led the Communist Party to power as the new leaders of China. Some, including my own grandparents with their children, feared the Communists and fled to the small offshore island of Taiwan. Many privileged Chinese chose to stay, however, motivated by a sincere belief that Mao Ze-dong would bring great changes to a nation weakened by centuries of corrupt government and foreign invasion.

And the Communists did alter China in many positive ways. Before Mao's liberation, my father remembers as a boy in the city of Shanghai seeing corpses of beggars lying in the streets while the wealthy drove by in chauffeured limousines. The Communists worked for the benefit of the poor, and united a nation shattered for decades into warring factions. Increasingly, however, it became clear that Mao Ze-dong, though an inspiring leader and brilliant revolutionary, was less skilled in the practical affairs of managing a country. Upon deciding that sparrows were harmful to the rice crop, for instance, Mao ordered the Chinese to hunt and kill them. While his directive did succeed in reducing the sparrow population, he had neglected to consider that birds also eat bugs; suddenly, the nation was besieged by a plague of insects.

By 1966 rivals such as President Liu Shao-qi were gaining power and influence within the Communist Party. At the same time, Mao himself had become disillusioned with some of the revolution's failures in transforming the nation. So the Cultural Revolution was born out of both Mao's genuine frustration and his desire to regain the upper hand in a power struggle that threatened his position. His call for "perpetual revolution" mobilized young people into Red Guards who would wage class war against remnants of traditional society, both native and foreign. Mao's strategy, however, ended up bringing untold suffering to those very masses in whose name the battle was waged, as well as disabling an entire group of young people who are now known as the "lost generation." Ironically, had Mao died before launching the Cultural Revolution, he would surely be remembered today as a much more positive historical figure.

Ji-li's story made me experience the Cultural Revolution on a gut level. Had I been born in China, I would have been nine years old in 1966, just a year younger than Ji-li's sister, Ji-yun. I too would have faced many of the same impossible choices: to slander a good teacher, or be labeled an enemy of the people? To reveal the location of a forbidden document, or risk its being discovered by the Red Guards? To betray my parents with lies, or ruin my own future?

Reading Ji-li's book, I believe I understand more deeply now what my distant uncle must have felt the day he lay down, thinking of his relatives in America, and snapped that photo. I can only hope I would have shown the same decency and courage exhibited by Ji-li Jiang. Her actions remind me that, even under unbearable circumstances, one can still believe in justice. And above all, love.

—David Henry Hwang

PROLOGUE

I was born on Chinese New Year.

Carefully, my parents chose my name: Ji-li, meaning lucky and beautiful. They hoped that I would be the happiest girl in the world.

And I was.

I was happy because I was always loved and respected. I was proud because I was able to excel and always expected to succeed. I was trusting, too. I never doubted what I was told: "Heaven and earth are great, but greater still is the kindness of the Communist Party; father and mother are dear, but dearer still is Chairman Mao."

With my red scarf, the emblem of the Young Pioneers, tied around my neck, and my heart bursting with joy, I achieved and grew every day until that fateful year, 1966.

That year I was twelve years old, in sixth grade.

That year the Cultural Revolution started.

THE LIBERATION ARMY DANCER

Chairman Mao, our beloved leader, smiled down at us from his place above the blackboard. The sounds and smells of the tantalizing May afternoon drifted in through the window. The sweet breeze carried the scent of new leaves and tender young grass and rippled the paper slogan below Chairman Mao's picture: STUDY HARD AND ADVANCE EVERY DAY. In the corner behind me the breeze also rustled the papers hanging from the Students' Garden, a beautifully decorated piece of cardboard that displayed exemplary work. One of them was my latest perfect math test.

We were having music class, but we couldn't keep our minds on the teacher's directions. We were all confused by the two-part harmony of the Young Pioneers' Anthem. "We are Young Pioneers, successors to Communism. Our red scarves flutter on our chests," we sang over and over, trying to get the timing right. The old black pump organ wheezed and squeaked as impatiently as we did. We made another start, but Wang Da-yong burst out a beat early, and the whole class broke into laughter.

Just then Principal Long appeared at the door. She walked in, looking less serious than usual, and behind her was a stranger, a beautiful young woman dressed in the People's Liberation Army uniform. A Liberation Army soldier! She was slim and stood straight as a reed. Her eyes sparkled, and her long braids, tied with red ribbons, swung at her waist. There was not a sound in the classroom as all forty of us stared at her in awe.

Principal Long told us to stand up. The woman soldier smiled but did not speak. She walked up and down the aisles, looking at us one by one. When she finished, she spoke quietly with Principal Long. "Tong Chao and Jiang Ji-li," Principal Long announced. "Come with us to the gym." A murmur rose behind us as we left the room. Tong Chao looked at me and I looked at him in wonder as we followed the swinging braids.

The gym was empty.

"I want to see how flexible you are. Let me lift your leg," the Liberation Army woman said in her gentle voice. She raised my right leg over my head in front of me. "Very good! Now I'll support you. Lean over backward as far as you can." That was easy. I bent backward until I could grab my ankles like an acrobat. "That's great!" she said, and her braids swung with excitement.

"This is Jiang Ji-li." Principal Long leaned forward proudly. "She's been studying martial arts since the second grade. She was on the Municipal Children's Martial Arts Team. Their demonstration was even filmed."

The Liberation Army woman smiled sweetly. "That was very good. Now you may go back to your classroom." She patted me on my head before she turned back to test Tong Chao.

I went back to class, but I could not remember the song we were singing. What did the Liberation Army woman want? Could she want to choose me for something? It was too much to contemplate. I hardly moved when the bell rang to end school. Someone told me that the principal wanted to see me. I walked slowly down the hall, surrounded by my shouting and jostling classmates, seeing only the beautiful soldier, feeling only the electric tingle of her soft touch on my head.

The office door was heavy. I pushed it open cautiously. Some students from the other sixth-grade classes were there already. I recognized Wang Qi, a girl in class two, and one of the boys, You Xiao-fan of class four. I didn't know the other boy. The three of them sat nervously and respectfully opposite Principal Long. I slipped into a chair next to them.

Principal Long leaned forward from her big desk. "I know you must be wondering about the Liberation Army soldier," she said. She sounded cheerful and excited. "Why did she come? Why did she want you to do back bends?" She looked at us one by one and then took a long sip from her tea mug as if she wanted to keep us guessing. "She was Comrade Li from the Central Liberation Army Arts Academy."

I slowly took a deep breath.

"She is recruiting students for the dance training class. She selected you four to audition. It's a great honor for Xin Er Primary School. I'm very proud of all of you, and I know you'll do your best."

I did not hear the rest of her words. I saw myself in a new Liberation Army uniform, slim and standing straight as a reed, long braids swinging at my waist. A Liberation Army soldier! One of the heroes admired by all, who helped Chairman Mao liberate China from oppression and defeated the Americans in Korea. And a performer, just like my mother used to be, touring the country, the world, to tell everyone about the New China that Chairman Mao had built and how it was becoming stronger and stronger.

I couldn't help giving Wang Qi a silly smile.

"Mom! Dad! Grandma!" I panted up the steep, dark stairs, in too much of a hurry to turn on the light, and tripped over some pots stored on the steps. I couldn't wait to tell them my news. I knew they would all be as excited as I was.

Our apartment was bright and warm and welcoming. Burgundy curtains shut the darkness outside and made the one big room even cozier. In front of the tall French window our square mahogany table was covered with steaming dishes and surrounded by my family, who were laughing and chattering when I rushed in. They all looked up expectantly.

"Everybody, guess what! Today a Liberation Army woman came to school and she tested me and she wants me to audition for the Central Liberation Army Arts Academy. Just think! I could be in the Liberation Army! And I could be a performer, too! Isn't it great?" I picked up our cat, Little White, and gave her a big kiss.

"It's lucky I studied martial arts for so long. When the Liberation Army woman saw my back bend, she just loved it." I twirled around on my toes and snapped my heels together in a salute. "Comrade Grandma, Jiang Ji-li reporting!"

My younger brother, Ji-yong, jumped up from the table and saluted me. My little sister, Ji-yun, started to twirl around as I had done, but she slipped and fell. We jumped to the floor with her and rolled around together.

"Ji-li," I heard Dad call. I looked up. Mom and Dad and Grandma were looking at each other solemnly. "It might be better not to do the audition." Dad spoke slowly, but his tone was serious, very serious.

"What?"

"Don't do the audition, Ji-li." He looked straight at me this time, and sounded much more forceful.

"Don't do the audition? Why not?"

Dad shook his head.

I grabbed Mom's arm. "Mom, why not?"

She squeezed my hand and looked at me worriedly. "Your father means that the recruitment requirements are very strict."

"Wow. You really scared me, Dad." I laughed with relief. "I know that. Principal Long told us it would be very competitive. I know it's just an audition, but who knows? I might be lucky, right?" I picked up a steamed bun and took a bite.

"I'm not just talking about talent," Dad said.

"There are more important requirements, political considerations . . ."

"Oh, Dad, that's no problem." I took another big bite of the bun. I was an Outstanding Student, an Excellent Young Pioneer, and even the *da-dui-zhang*, the student chairman of the whole school. What more could they want? My mouth was full, so I stretched out my arm to show Dad my *da-dui-zhang* badge, a plastic tag with three red stripes.

I saw a pain in Dad's eyes that I had never seen before.

"The problem isn't with you yourself, Ji-li. What I mean is that the political background investigations at these academies are very severe."

"Political background investigation? What's that?"

"That is an investigation into the class status of your ancestors and all members of your family." He leaned back in his chair, and the lampshade put his face in shadow. "Ji-li, the fact is that our family will not be able to pass these investigations," he said slowly. "And you will not be allowed to be a member of a Liberation Army performing troupe."

For a long time I did not speak. "Why?" I whispered at last.

He started to say something but stopped. He leaned

forward again, and I could see the sorrow on his face. "It's very complicated, and you wouldn't understand it now even if I told you. Maybe we should wait until you're grown up. The point is that I don't think you'll be admitted. So just drop it, all right?"

I did not say anything. Putting down the half-eaten bun, I walked to the mirror on the big wardrobe that divided the room and pressed my forehead against its cool surface. I could not hold back any longer. I burst out crying.

"I want to do it. I want to try. What will I tell Principal Long? And my classmates?" I wailed.

"Maybe we should let her try. She probably won't be chosen anyway." Grandma looked at Dad.

Dad stood up, heaving a deep sigh. "This is for her own good. Her classmates and teachers will just be surprised if she says that her father won't let her go. But what if she passes the audition and can't pass the political background investigation? Then everybody will know that the family has a political problem." Dad's voice grew louder and louder as he went on.

Ji-yong and Ji-yun were looking up at Dad, wide-eyed. I bit my lip to force myself to stop crying and went to bed without saying another word.

★ ★ ★

The hallway outside the principal's office was very quiet. It was noon, and nearly everyone was home for lunch. The big red characters PRINCIPAL'S OFFICE made me nervous. I put my hand on the knob, hesitated, and lowered it. I walked back to the stairs, trembling and covered with sweat.

I rehearsed the words I was going to say one more time. Then I rushed back to the office door and pushed it open.

Principal Long was reading a newspaper. She raised her head and peered through her glasses to see who had interrupted her. "Principal Long, here is a note from my father." Hastily I gave her the note, damp with sweat from my palm. I hurried out of the office before she could look at it or ask me any questions. I ran down the hallway, colliding with someone and running blindly on, thinking only that she must be very disappointed.

At one o'clock when the bell finally rang to start class, I heaved a long sigh and walked out of the library. My best friend, An Yi, and our homeroom teacher were standing outside the main building. As soon as they saw me, An Yi shouted, "Where have you been? Aren't you supposed to go to the audition at one? Hurry up! You're going to be late."

I opened my mouth but couldn't say a word.

"Why, what's wrong?" Teacher Gu asked.

"I . . . I'm not going." I bowed my head and twisted my fingers in my red scarf.

"What? Are you crazy? This is the chance of a lifetime!"

I did not raise my head. I didn't want to see An Yi's face.

"Really? Why not?" Teacher Gu sounded concerned.

I tried hard not to cry. "Father wouldn't let me. . . ."

An Yi was about to say something else, but Teacher Gu cut her off. "All right. This is her family's decision. We won't talk about it any further." She put her hand on my shoulder and gave me a little squeeze. Then she went away with An Yi without another word.

Across the yard I saw Principal Long, Wang Qi, and the two boys coming out of the gym. I dodged behind a tree and heard them chatting and laughing as they went by. They were going to the audition. I could have been going with them. My eyes blurred with tears.

I thought of the way Teacher Gu had looked at me. There had been a mixture of disappointment, doubt, and inquiry in her eyes. I was sure that Principal Long must have looked the same way after she read Dad's note. So must Wang Qi, You Xiao-fan, and all my classmates.

I didn't want to think any longer. I just wished that I could find a place to hide, so I wouldn't have to see their faces.

Until that spring I believed that my life and my family were nearly perfect.

My father was a stage actor, six feet tall and slightly stoop shouldered. Because of his height and his serious face he usually played the villain at the children's theater where he worked. He was the vicious landlord, the foolish king. But at home he was our humorous, kind, and wise Dad. He loved reading, and he loved including the whole family in his discoveries. He demonstrated the exercises of the great acting teacher Stanislavsky, he imitated Charlie Chaplin's funny walk, and when he was reading about calculus, he explained Zeno's paradox and the infinite series. We thought Dad knew everything.

Mom had been an actress when she met Dad, and she was still as pretty as an actress. When I was little, she stopped acting and worked in a sports-equipment store. Every evening we eagerly waited for her to come home from work. We rushed out to greet her and opened her handbag, where there was sure to be a treat for us. Mom spoiled us, Grandma said.

Grandma was truly amazing. She had graduated

from a modern-style high school in 1914, a time when very few girls went to school at all. After Liberation she had helped to found Xin Er Primary School—my school—and become its vice-principal. She retired from teaching when I was born so that she could take care of me while Mom worked. But whenever we met her old students, now adults, they still bowed respectfully and called her Teacher Cao, which made me so proud.

Ji-yong was eleven, one year younger than me, and Ji-yun was one year younger than Ji-yong. Once Mom told me that she had her three children in three years because she wanted to finish the duty of having babies sooner, so she could devote herself wholeheartedly to the revolution. While I was tall and thin, like Dad, Ji-yong and Ji-yun were shorter and plumper, like Mom. Ji-yong was nicknamed Iron-Ball because he was dark skinned and sturdy. He liked to play in the alley and paid little attention to his studies. Ji-yun had two dimples, which gave her an especially sweet smile. She was easygoing and did not always strive to be the best, as I did. But I had learned that she could be very stubborn.

And then there was Song Po-po. She had originally been our nanny. When we grew up, she stayed and became our housekeeper. As long as I could remember, she had been living in the small room downstairs. She had raised the three of us, and we all felt she was like another grandmother. She was as dear to us as we were to her.

We lived in a big building in one of Shanghai's nicer neighborhoods. My Fourth Aunt, who had been married to Dad's half-brother, lived downstairs with her daughter, my cousin You-mei, and You-mei's daughter, a lovely baby called Hua-hua. My uncle had died in Hong Kong a few years before. You-mei's husband had a job in another city and was allowed to visit Shanghai only twice a year.

Song Po-po told us our extended family used to occupy two whole buildings, ten rooms all together. "Then they all moved away, and only your family and your Fourth Aunt's family were left. Your family only has one room now. It's just too bad." She shook her head sadly.

But I didn't feel that way at all. I loved our top-floor room. A huge French window and a high ceiling made it bright all year round, warmer during the winter and cooler in summer. The kitchen on the landing outside the room was small, but I didn't mind. Our room was ten times as big as many of my classmates' homes, and a hundred times brighter. Best of all, we had a private bathroom, a full-size room with a sink, a toilet, and a tub. It was almost as large as some families' entire homes. Many did not have a bathroom at all, or even a flush toilet, and very few had a full-size bathroom that they did not have to share with other families.

My family was also special in another way.

Sometimes on Saturday evenings some of Dad's colleagues would visit. They called these gatherings "Jiang's salon." I did not know what *salon* meant, but I loved them; they were wonderful parties. Mom would make her famous beef soup, and Grandma would make her steamed buns. We children would help Song Po-po polish the mahogany table and Grandma's four prized red-and-gold dowry trunks until we could see our reflections in the wood and leather. When the guests arrived, we would greet them as "Uncle" and "Aunt" as a sign of respect and bring tea to each of them. Most of them were actors from Dad's theater, and they were all talented. There was Uncle Zhu, a young actor who had excellent handwriting. Every time he came, he would take some time to help me with my calligraphy. There were Uncle Tian and Aunt Wu, so young and handsome and well dressed that the neighbors noticed every time they rolled up to our building on their new bicycles, and called them the "beautiful couple." There was Uncle Fan, who had been Dad's friend since college.

When he arrived, the discussions immediately became more interesting. His enthusiasm about whatever movie or play he had seen recently was contagious. And there was Uncle Bao, a playwright, who smoked cigars and let me sit on his lap. Although he spoke less than the others, his comments were always worth waiting for.

Conversation flowed, so fascinating that we did not want to go to bed, no matter how late they stayed.

Until the audition I felt like the luckiest girl in the world.

An Yi said that I seemed to have changed into a different person. Between classes I would avoid my classmates. After school I would stay in the library until it closed, just to elude the family's overconcerned looks.

One time our cat, Little White, cut her leg deeply on a piece of glass. We all rushed to find bandages to bind up the wound, but Little White ran into the attic and hid there for days, licking her wounds by herself. Just like Little White, I wanted to be left alone.

None of the other three students passed the audition, but this did not make me feel better. It had not been just an audition for me. I was afraid that the rest of my life would not be what I had imagined.

I had had many beautiful dreams. I dreamed of

being a doctor in a white coat, with a stethoscope dangling from my neck, saving lives one after another. I dreamed of being an architect, designing the most beautiful bridges in the world. I dreamed of being an actress, holding bunches of flowers, bowing again and again to answer curtain calls. Until now I had never doubted that I could achieve anything I wanted. The future had been full of infinite possibilities. Now I was no longer sure that was still true.

One afternoon, a week after the audition, I came home from school and saw a boy blowing big, splendid soap bubbles that shimmered with colors in the sunlight. One by one they drifted away and burst. In a few seconds they were all gone.

I thought about my beautiful dreams and wondered if they would drift away just like those lovely soap bubbles.

DESTROY THE
FOUR OLDS!

Almost every Sunday afternoon Dad wanted to take a long nap in peace, and so he gave us thirty fen to rent picture books. Hand in hand, Ji-yong, Ji-yun, and I would walk down the alley to Grandpa Hong's bookstall.

The alley on which we lived was famous for its handsome buildings, and it was wide enough for two cars to pass abreast. Like a tree with only one trunk, our alley had only one exit to the busy street. Five smaller alleys branched off the main alley on both sides, and each of these small alleys was lined with brownstone town houses. The houses were three stories tall and exactly alike, with square, smiling courtyards hidden behind their front gates, and small kitchen courtyards in the back. Once these had been town houses for wealthy families. Many of the original inhabitants still lived there, although now each building was shared by several families.

Grandpa Hong's bookstall was on the corner at the entrance of our alley. All the children in the neighborhood loved the stall and Grandpa Hong, with his gray hair and wispy beard. He would look at us through his old yellowed glasses and smile. He knew just which books each of us liked best and that I would choose fairy tales, Ji-yong would get adventure stories, and Ji-yun would want animal stories. If you read the books at Grandpa Hong's bookstall, you could rent sixty picture books for thirty fen. Two books for a fen! What a deal! After helping us with our choices, Grandpa Hong always gave us each an extra book for free.

Against the walls in the place were hard wooden benches that rocked on the uneven mud floor. We would sit in a row on one of these benches, each of us with a pile of twenty-one picture books, and read them, one after another. Then we would trade piles and read again. This was how I met many beloved friends: the Monkey King, the River Snail Lady, Snow White, Aladdin, and many others. Inside the bookstall I traveled to mysterious places to meet ancient beauties or terrible monsters. Often I forgot where I was. When the sky was almost dark, the three of us would have finished all sixty-three books, and Dad would have finished his nap.

This Sunday there were no other children at the stall

when we arrived. We had just settled down to read when An Yi rushed in. An Yi and I had known each other ever since we were babies. She came to the bookstall quite often and knew just where to find me on a Sunday afternoon.

"Come on, you guys!" she wheezed. An Yi had severe asthma. "They're breaking the sign at the Great Prosperity Market!"

We dropped our books and rushed out with her. This was our first chance to watch the campaign to "Destroy the Four Olds" in action.

Our beloved Chairman Mao had started the Cultural Revolution in May. Every day since then on the radio we heard about the need to end the evil and pernicious influences of the "Four Olds": old ideas, old culture, old customs, and old habits. Chairman Mao told us we would never succeed at building a strong socialist country until we destroyed the "Four Olds" and established the "Four News." The names of many shops still stank of old culture, so the signs had to be smashed to make way for the coming of new ideas.

The Great Prosperity Market was on Nanjing Road, Shanghai's busiest shopping street, only two blocks from our alley. Nanjing Road was lined with big stores, and always bustled with activity. The street was full of bicycles and pedicabs and trolleys, and the sidewalks were so crowded with shoppers, they spilled off the sidewalk into the street. We were still quite a distance away when we heard the hubbub and ran faster.

A big crowd had gathered outside the Great Prosperity Market, one of the most successful food stores in the city. It was full of good things to eat, with rare delicacies from other provinces and delicious items like dried duck gizzards strung up in its window. But today the window was bare. The store was deserted. All eyes were riveted on a dense ring of people in the street. Some young men were cheering excitedly for the people inside the circle, but half the crowd were merely craning their necks and watching.

We wriggled our way between the bodies.

Lying on the dirty ground inside the circle was a huge wooden sign, at least twelve feet long. It was still impressive, although the large golden characters GREAT PROSPERITY MARKET had lost their usual shine and looked dull and lifeless on the red background.

Two muscular young men in undershirts, probably salesmen from the store, were gasping next to it.

"Come on. Try again!" shouted the taller of the two.

He spat into his palms and rubbed them together.

Then, with the help of the other, he lifted the board to shoulder height. "One, two, three!" They threw the board to the ground.

The board bounced twice but did not break. The two men threw the board again. Nothing happened.

"Put one end on the curb. Stamp on it. That's bound to work," someone suggested.

"Good idea!"

"Come on! Try it!"

Amid a clamor of support, the two men moved the board half onto the sidewalk. Then they jumped onto it. "One . . . two . . . three . . ." We heard their shoes strike the hard wood. But the board did not yield.

"Damn! This fourolds is really hard. Hey! Come on. Let's do it together!" the tall fellow shouted at the crowd.

I looked at An Yi to see if she would like to join me, but while I was hesitating, the board became fully occupied. Ji-yong had moved faster and was one of the dozen people on it. They stamped, bounced, and jumped with excitement. One stepped on another's shoes. Hips and shoulders bumped. We all laughed.

The board refused to break. Even under a thousand pounds it did not give way. The crowd became irritated and started shouting suggestions.

"Take it to a carpenter and let him use it for something!"

"Let's get a truck and drive over it!"

Someone started pushing through the circle.

"Hey, I've got an ax. Let me through! I've got an ax!"

We stood back to give the man room. He lifted the ax to his shoulder and paused. The blade flashed in the sunlight as it began to move faster and faster in a shining arc until it crashed into the sign. The wood groaned with the impact, and we all cheered. The man gave the sign another blow, and another. At last the sign gave way. With another groan and a crack it broke in two.

Everyone cheered. People rushed forward to stamp on what remained of the sign. An Yi and I had found a few classmates in the crowd, and we all embraced, jumped, and shouted. Although what we had smashed was no more than a piece of wood, we felt we had won a victory in a real battle.

Bathed in the evening's glow, we jumped and giggled all the way home. Inspired by what we'd seen, we noticed that other stores we passed also needed to change their names.

"Look. This is called the Good Fortune Photo Studio. Doesn't that mean to make a lot of money, just like Great Prosperity? Chairman Mao told us that was exploitation. Don't you think this is fourolds?" Ji-yong asked enthusiastically.

"Right. We should change it to the Proletarian Photo Studio."

"Here's another one. The Innocent Child Toy Shop," An Yi exclaimed. "*Innocent* is a neutral word. It shows a lack of class awareness. What should we change it to?"

"How about the Red Child Toy Shop?"

"That's great," I said. "And we should change the Peace Theater to the Revolution Theater. After all, without revolution, how can we have peace?"

We felt proud of ourselves. We were certain that we were bringing a new life to China.

So Grandma's reaction was a surprise to me. At dinner I told her and my parents all about what had happened.

"My goodness!" she blurted out. "That sign cost the owner a fortune. They always said that since an especially auspicious date was chosen to hang the sign, the store has been prosperous for more than thirty years. What a shame! What a shame!"

"But Grandma, we have to get rid of those old ideas, old culture, old customs, and old habits. Chairman Mao said they're holding us back," I informed her.

"Besides, Grandma, there's no such thing as an auspicious date. That's superstition, and superstition is fourolds. And the name Great Prosperity is very bad. Great prosperity means to make a fortune, and making a fortune is what bad people do. Right?" Ji-yong tilted his head toward Mom and Dad.

Mom and Dad looked at each other and then turned to Grandma.

"Yes, Ji-yong is right," Mom said, and shook her head.

Even my little sister, Ji-yun, knew that the old superstitions were silly. Like not sweeping the floor on New Year's Day so you would not sweep the god of wealth out of the house, or eating a spring roll so you would roll the money in. I told Grandma what I had heard from my classmates. "An Yi said her uncle knew a family who spent a lot of money when their grandma died. First they had to keep vigil by the coffin for a week. Then after the burial they had to have a banquet and serve bean curd to the relatives every seventh day for seven weeks, and on the forty-ninth day they had the last banquet, all just so the soul could get into heaven. Then they burned spirit money so that the dead person would have money in heaven. What good does all that do? Besides, there is no such thing as heaven. It's

26

these old ideas that are holding the country back."

Ji-yong and Ji-yun and I talked about the new shop names we had thought of. Mom and Dad did not say anything. They did not seem very enthusiastic about the new campaign. That was surprising, because they had been very enthusiastic about previous movements. When I was little, Chairman Mao had challenged the nation to catch up with England and America in steel production. Mom had helped me collect scrap iron to make steel, and even let me donate our cast-iron kettle to the cause. When natural disasters had caused food shortages, Chairman Mao had urged us all to produce food. Mom had helped me grow pots of seaweed on the balcony, as all my classmates did. Chairman Mao's campaign to "Destroy the Four Olds" was even more important than the others. The newspapers and the radio said so. I knew the movement was vital to our country's future, and I did not understand how Mom and Dad could not be interested in it.

It was almost unbelievable. Within a couple of days almost all the fourolds shop signs had been removed. The stores we had talked about had all been renamed. Red banners now hung over the doorways as temporary signs, with the new names painted in black or white. The red cloths were not as nice as the old signs, but their revolutionary spirit brought a new energy to the whole city. It seemed to me that the very air had become purer with the change.

What excited me and my friends most, though, was that the Peace Theater really did become the Revolution Theater, as we had said it should. We felt like real revolutionaries at last.

My friends and I had grown up with the stories of the brave revolutionaries who had saved China. We were proud of our precious red scarves, which, like the national flag, were dyed red with the blood of our revolutionary martyrs. We had often been sorry that we were too young to have fought with Chairman Mao against the Japanese invaders, who tried to conquer China; against the dictator Chiang Kai-shek, who ruthlessly oppressed the Chinese people; and against the American aggressors in Korea. We had missed our chance to become national heroes by helping our motherland.

Now our chance had come. Destroying the fourolds was a new battle, and an important one: It would keep China from losing her Communist ideals. Though we were not facing real guns or real tanks, this battle would be even harder, because our enemies, the rotten ideas and customs we were so used to, were inside ourselves.

I was so excited that I forgot my sadness about the audition. There were many more important missions waiting for me. I felt I was already a Liberation Army soldier who was ready to go out for battle.

Ji-yun and I were walking home. The street was crowded with the bicycles of people coming home from work and with electric trolley buses blowing horns and crammed with passengers.

As usual, Ji-yun had not done very well at her piano lesson. "You have to pay attention to your teacher," I was telling her. "He told you to slow down when you got to the end of the last verse, but you sped up. I don't know what's wrong with you. Now, what did he say about the new piece? What kind of mood is it?"

"Happy?" Ji-yun guessed.

I sighed. "He said it was stirring. That's a lot more than just happy. You have to pay attention. You really embarrass me. You—"

The sight of some high school students distracted me. Two boys and a pigtailed girl were walking toward us. They were young, no more than three or four years older than me. They walked slowly through the bustling crowd, looking closely at people's pants and shoes. My sister and I stared at them with admiration. We knew they must be student inspectors. The newspapers had pointed out that the fourolds were also reflected in clothing, and now high school students had taken responsibility for eliminating such dress. For example, any pants with a leg narrower than eight inches for women or nine inches for men would be considered fourolds.

A bus pulled up at the bus stop behind us. Quite a few people got on and off. As the bus pulled away, we saw a crowd gathered at the curb. "Oh boy, they found a target." I took Ji-yun by the hand and dashed over.

". . . tight pants and pointed shoes are what the Western bourgeoisie admire. For us proletarians they are neither good-looking nor comfortable. What's more, they are detrimental to the revolution, so we must oppose them resolutely." One of the boys, the one who was wearing glasses, was just finishing his speech.

The guilty person was a very handsome man in his early thirties. He wore dark-framed glasses, a cream-colored jacket with the zipper half open, and a pair of sharply creased light-brown pants. He had also been wearing fashionable two-tone shoes, "champagne shoes" we called them, of cream and light-brown leather. They were lying on the ground next to him as he stood with one foot on the ground and the other resting in the lap of the student measuring his pants.

The man kept arching his foot as if the pebbles on the sidewalk hurt him. He looked nervous, standing in his white socks while the inspectors surrounded him, holding his hands submissively along his trouser seams. Occasionally he raised his hands a little to balance himself. His handsome face blushed scarlet, then turned pale. A few times he bit his lips.

One of the boys was trying to squeeze an empty beer bottle up the man's trouser leg. This was a newly invented measurement. If the bottle could not be stuffed into the trouser leg, the pants were considered fourolds and treated with "revolutionary operations"— cut open.

The boy tried twice. The girl waved her scissors with unconcealed delight. "Look! Another pair of too-tight pants. Now let's get rid of the fourolds!" She raised the scissors and deftly cut the pants leg open. Then, with both hands, she tore the pants to the knee so the man's pale calf was exposed.

The crowd stirred. Some people pushed forward to have a closer look, some nervously left the circle when they saw the scissors used, and some glanced at their own pants. As the girl started on the other leg of the trousers, the boy with the glasses picked up the man's shoes and waved them to the crowd. "Pointed shoes! Fourolds!" he shouted.

"But I bought them in the Number One Department Store here. It's run by the government. How can they be fourolds?" the man cried out in despair.

"What makes you think that government-owned stores are free of fourolds? That statement itself is fourolds. Didn't you see all the shop signs that were knocked down? Most of those stores belonged to the government." With a snort the boy dropped the man's foot and stood up. The man lost his balance and nearly fell over.

The crowd gave a burst of appreciative laughter.

Encouraged, the three students enthusiastically began cutting open the shoes. All eyes were focused on them. No one paid any attention to their owner. I looked at the man.

He stood on the sidewalk, awkward and humiliated, trouser legs flapping around his ankles, socks falling down. A tuft of hair hung over his forehead. He looked at his pants, pushed up his glasses nervously, and quickly glanced around. Our eyes met. Immediately he turned away.

The students cheered and triumphantly threw the mutilated shoes into the air.

The man quivered. Suddenly he turned around and began to walk away.

"Wait." One boy picked up the shoes and threw them at the man. "Take your fourolds with you. Go home and thoroughly remold your ideology."

The man took his broken shoes in hand and made his way out of the crowd, his cut pants flapping.

Someone chortled. "He'll have holes in his socks when he gets home."

I watched the spectators disperse. The students strutted proudly down the street.

Ji-yun tugged on my arm. "Come on. It's over."

I took her hand and we headed home in silence. "That poor guy," I finally said. "He should know better than to dress that way, but I'd just die if somebody cut my pants open in front of everybody like that."

School had just let out. No sooner had we left the classroom than the rain began to pour down in huge drops. Those of us who hadn't brought umbrellas scurried back into the classroom.

"Gosh! I should have brought my *yang-san* like

Mom told me to." An Yi gasped for breath while brushing the rain off her clothes.

"An Yi, you're spreading the fourolds." Yang Fan popped up behind her and spoke half jokingly. I was surprised. Yang Fan was usually so hesitant to express an opinion of her own that we called her Echo.

"What? What do you mean?" An Yi asked indignantly.

"You just said *yang-san* for 'umbrella.' Isn't that spreading the fourolds?"

"Are you kidding? If *yang-san* is fourolds, then what about 'raincoat'?"

Several other classmates laughed and gathered around An Yi and Yang Fan.

Yang Fan's smile faded into embarrassment.

"What's so funny? That *is* fourolds." Du Hai stepped onto a chair and sat heavily on a desk. "*Yang* means foreign. *Yang-san* means foreign umbrella. They were called that because before Liberation we had to import them. Now we make them in China. So why do you still call it a *yang-san*? Doesn't that show that you're a xenophile who worships anything foreign?" Du Hai reveled in the new phrase he had learned from the newspaper.

Du Hai was trouble. He was mischievous and a

terrible student, but he was hard to beat in an argument. Most important of all, his mother was the Neighborhood Party Committee Secretary, and so no one wanted to offend him.

He looked at us and we looked at him.

"First of all, this *yang* means sun, not foreign. And this *yang-san* means sun umbrella, parasol, not foreign umbrella." I didn't even look at Du Hai while I corrected his mistake. "If you want to talk about fourolds, Yang Fan, you always say *yang-huo* for matches. That really does mean foreign fire. So aren't you spreading the fourolds too?" I sneaked a glance at Du Hai as I supported An Yi. Everyone laughed.

Yang Fan did not expect my attack and was caught short. She looked to Du Hai for help.

"Well, you always say good morning and good afternoon to the teachers." Du Hai struck back. "That's fourolds too, don't you know that?"

"What's wrong with saying good morning to the teachers? They teach you and you should respect them," An Yi fired back before I could stop her.

"Respect the teachers? That's the nonsense of 'teachers' dignity.' You two are typical 'teachers' obedient little lambs,' do you know that?" Du Hai recited more phrases from the newspaper.

The world had turned upside down. Now it was a crime for students to respect teachers. I couldn't keep calm.

"We're 'teachers' obedient little lambs,' are we? Well, what about you, Du Hai? You're full of the fourolds. On the last arithmetic test you only got twenty-six out of a hundred, and you said that your stupidity was due to your sins in a former life. Isn't that what you said? Isn't reincarnation a superstition?" I raised my voice.

"And you also said that the fortune-teller told you 'small eyes, large fortune.' Isn't that fourolds too?" An Yi kept pressing hard.

Du Hai's tiny, squinty eyes got even smaller. "That . . . that was just a joke. Anyway, I'm not as full of the fourolds as you are. You always say, 'Listen to the teachers, listen to your parents.'" He wheezed in an expert imitation of An Yi, and all of our classmates burst into laughter. Du Hai and Yang Fan looked immensely pleased with themselves.

"Jiang Ji-li, your family has a housekeeper. That is exploitation. You're a capitalist."

"An Yi, you use facial cream every day. That is bourgeois ideology. And your long hair is, too. Shame on you. Why don't you get your hair cut short in a revolutionary style?"

Du Hai and Yang Fan took turns attacking us, so quickly and fiercely that An Yi and I did not have a chance to reply. Everyone laughed at our helplessness.

"Well, the rain's stopped. Let's go home." Feeling they had the upper hand and wanting to quit while they were ahead, Du Hai and Yang Fan picked up their schoolbags and swaggered off. The rest of the crowd followed them out, still shouting with laughter.

We two were left alone, angry and helpless.

"What's wrong with using skin cream and wearing a braid?" said An Yi, stamping hard on the ground.

"But maybe they're right about the housekeeper," I admitted as we slung our schoolbags over our shoulders. "I guess I'll have to tell Mom what they said about Song Po-po."

WRITING DA-ZI-BAO

Who would have believed that our entire educational system was wrong after all? Seventeen years after Liberation, the newspapers told us, our schools were not bringing us up to be good red socialists and communists, as we had thought, but revisionists. We thanked heaven that Chairman Mao had started this Cultural Revolution, and that the Central Committee of the Communist Party had uncovered the mess in our schools. Otherwise we would not even have known that we were in trouble. What a frightening idea!

One Monday, all school classes were suspended indefinitely. All students were directed instead to participate in the movement by writing big posters, *da-zi-bao*, criticizing the educational system. Rolls of white paper, dozens of brushes, and many bottles of red and black ink were brought into the classrooms. The teachers were nowhere to be seen.

The classrooms buzzed with revolutionary fervor.

Students spread large sheets of paper on desks and gathered around, eagerly shouting suggestions. Some roamed the rooms, reading comments aloud over people's shoulders, calling to others. Girls and boys ran outside to put up their *da-zi-bao* and ran back in to write more. Desks, Ping-Pong tables, and even the floor were taken over for writing *da-zi-bao*. When the white paper was gone, the students used old newspaper instead. *Da-zi-bao* were everywhere: in classrooms, along the hallways, and even on the brick walls of the school yard. The row of tall parasol trees that lined the inside of the school yard was festooned with more *da-zi-bao*, hanging like flowers from the branches. Long ropes strung across the playground were covered with still more *da-zi-bao*, looking like laundry hung out to dry.

I stared at the large sheet of paper spread out in front of me, wondering what to write. It was strange. When I had read the newspaper, I had been enraged by the revisionist educational system that had been poisoning our youth for so many years. But now that I actually had to criticize the teachers who taught us every day, I could not find anything really bad to say about any of them.

I went over to An Yi's desk. Just as I guessed, the

papers in front of her and her seatmate, Zhang Jie, were also blank.

"I just can't think of anything to write," I complained.

"Neither can we. I might as well just give up." An Yi put her brush down and stretched.

"Hey, everybody has to write something. You're no exception. Do you want everyone to think you have a bad political attitude?" Zhang Jie was joking, but it made us think.

"Why don't we go out to the playground to see what everybody else is writing?" Zhang Jie went on. "It's better to copy something than not to write anything at all. What do you say?"

We walked out to the school yard. The classroom had been crowded, but there were even more students outside. Du Hai was shouting, "Hey, this is great! Everybody, look at what Pauper's done. She put the principal's name upside down."

Ragged-looking Pauper smiled with satisfaction. "I saw my big sister writing one last night. She wrote the name upside down and then put a big red X over it. She said that's what the court used to do to criminals."

The three of us stopped before a *da-zi-bao* signed "An Antirevisionist." An Yi read aloud, "'Although teachers do not hold bombs or knives, they are still dangerous enemies. They fill us with insidious revisionist ideas. They teach us that scholars are superior to workers. They promote personal ambition by encouraging competition for the highest grades. All these things are intended to change good young socialists into corrupt revisionists. They are invisible knives that are even more dangerous than real knives or guns. For example, a student from Yu-cai High School killed himself because he failed the university entrance examination. Brainwashed by his teachers, he believed his sole aim in life was to enter a famous university and become a scientist—"

"Hey!" I stopped her in surprise. "This was all copied from the *Youth Post*. I read it the other day."

"So what? It's always okay to copy *da-zi-bao*," Zhang Jie said. She turned to another *da-zi-bao*. "Look! This one is by Yin Lan-lan."

Yin Lan-lan had written, "As one of its victims, I denounce the revisionist educational system. Being from a working class family, I have to do a lot more housework than students from rich families. So I have difficulty passing exams. I was forced to repeat grades three times. And I was not allowed to be a Young Pioneer or to participate in the school choir. The teachers think only of grades when evaluating a student.

They forget that we, the working class, are the masters of our socialist country."

"Yin Lan-lan? A victim?" I was flabbergasted. Yin Lan-lan had flunked three times. She rarely spoke up in class. When she was asked to answer a question, she would just stand there without saying a word. She was not very bright.

"She failed three courses out of five. How could she blame the teachers for that?" An Yi sneered.

Zhang Jie slumped her shoulders and bowed her head in imitation of Yin Lan-lan. We burst out laughing and immediately looked around to see if anyone was watching us. Zhang Jie made a face.

Sheet after sheet, article after article, each *da-zi-bao* was a bitter accusation. One was titled, "Teacher Li, Abuser of the Young." The student had failed to hand in her homework on time, and Teacher Li had told her to copy the assignment over five times as punishment. Another student said his teacher had deliberately ruined his students' eyesight by making them read a lot, so they could not join the Liberation Army. Still another accused Teacher Wang of attempting to corrupt a young revolutionary by buying her some bread when he learned that she had not eaten lunch.

The more I read, the more puzzled I became. Did

the teachers really intend to ruin our health and corrupt our minds? If so, why hadn't I ever noticed? Was I so badly taken in that I was unable to see them for what they really were? I remembered Du Hai's taunt. *You "teachers' obedient little lamb."* I thought of Teacher Gu, who was like a stern but loving mother to me. I thought of An Yi's mother, Teacher Wei, who had won so many Model Teacher awards because of her dedication to her work. No matter how I tried, I just could not relate them to the villains described in the *da-zi-bao*.

To fulfill my responsibility as a revolutionary, I listed all my teachers. One by one, I considered them carefully. Unfortunately, none of them seemed to hate the Party or oppose Chairman Mao. I could not write a *da-zi-bao* about any of them.

Finally I decided to copy an article from the newspaper instead.

A few days later, when I got to school, I was told we were going to post *da-zi-bao* on the houses of some of the bourgeoisie living near the school. The class was divided into two groups. One was going to confront Old Qian, a stern and frightening man who stalked our alleys speaking to no one. The other group was going to challenge Jiang Xi-wen, an unpleasant woman who lived in a house behind the school yard. I was assigned to the group going to Jiang Xi-wen's house. Of course, this was not coincidence, not at all. They all knew that she was my relative.

Aunt Xi-wen was really my father's cousin, but I always called her Aunt. She was at least fifty years old, but she dressed stylishly and wore makeup, so she looked closer to thirty. I knew my classmates did not like her one bit. "What makes her think she's so wonderful?" they sneered. "Just look at those clothes she got from her sister in America. Look at her makeup. Bourgeois! Disgusting!" I had always disapproved of her too. Chairman Mao taught us that "inner beauty is much more valuable than outward appearance." How could she ignore what Chairman Mao said? Song Po-po had told me that even Aunt Xi-wen's youngest son often grumbled about his mother's behavior.

Just a few weeks earlier Aunt Xi-wen had complained to the school because some students had climbed into her yard to pick mulberry leaves for their silkworms. This latest affront was too much for the students to bear.

About twenty of us formed a straggling column. Yin Lan-lan was first in line. She carried the *da-zi-bao*, and Du Hai, carrying a brush and a bucket of paste, followed her. Behind them two students struck a gong and beat a drum.

"Let's go!" Yin Lan-lan waved her arm vigorously, and the group marched off.

I watched her with interest. Yin Lan-lan had changed a great deal. No longer hesitant and clumsy, she had become vocal, aggressive, and confident. She stood up straight and threw out her chest, whereas before she had always slouched. She and Du Hai had taken the leading roles in this movement. The usual leaders of the class, including me, were holding back for some reason. Yu Jian, chairman of the class and one of the best students, was somewhere in the middle of the line, while I dawdled so that I could be in the back of the group. I didn't want Aunt Xi-wen to see me. Although I did not approve of her, and although I supported today's revolutionary action, she was still my relative. But I dared not ask to switch to the other group. I would certainly be criticized for letting my family relationships interfere with my political principles. I had no choice but to go.

Someone rang the bell. We waited in the narrow passageway outside the door, whispering among ourselves. Before long Aunt Xi-wen came to the door. She was not wearing makeup, and she looked older and less attractive than usual. She seemed taken aback at the sight of us. Her welcoming expression turned into one of nervous surprise.

Du Hai took the lead. "Down with the bourgeois Jiang Xi-wen! Long live Mao Ze-dong Thought!" he shouted. We repeated the slogans. Then Yin Lan-lan recited, "Our great leader, Chairman Mao, has taught us, 'Every reactionary is the same; if you do not hit him, he will not fall. This is also like sweeping the floor; as a rule, where the broom does not reach, the dust will not vanish by itself.'" Her voice was loud and forceful. "Today, we proletarian revolutionary young guards have come to revolt against you bourgeoisie. Jiang Xi-wen, this is our *da-zi-bao*. You are to post it on your door now." She shook the white paper in front of Aunt Xi-wen's nose.

Aunt Xi-wen tried to smile to show her support of the proletarian revolutionary young guards, but the smile froze before it was fully formed. It was hard to tell whether she was smiling or crying.

"Yes, yes, I will," she said repeatedly. She took the paste and began to brush it on the door. I could see the brush quivering in her hand. It was an unusually hot and humid day, and with the twenty of us crowded into her entryway, it felt even hotter. Aunt Xi-wen gave the door a few more good swipes of paste before she stopped and wiped the sweat off her forehead. Then she took the *da-zi-bao* and stuck it to the door, smoothing it out without hesitation in spite of the ink that blacked her hands.

"Now read it out loud," Yin Lan-lan shouted as soon as Aunt Xi-wen finished.

Aunt Xi-wen had not expected this. She gaped at us in alarm. She did not want to read the terrible things written about her, but she did not dare refuse. Her face was ugly with distress. She knew that no one would challenge anything we revolutionaries did to her.

I did not want her to see me. I bent down and pretended to tie my shoelaces. But I could not block out her voice, dry, hoarse, and trembling: " . . . refusal to let students pick mulberry leaves was an attack on proletarian students. . . . The more you try to improve your outward appearance, the filthier your heart becomes. . . . Your black bourgeois bones are clearly visible to our proletarian eyes. . . . Remold yourself conscientiously. . . ." I kept my eyes on my shoelaces and tried not to listen.

"Hey, what's the matter with you?" Someone pushed me and I realized that it was over.

On the way back to school everyone joked and

47

laughed at Aunt Xi-wen's humiliation. "Jiang Ji-li, your aunt really lost face today, didn't she?" Du Hai shouted. I could feel every classmate staring at me. I raised my head and said loudly, "It serves her right." I made an effort to laugh and joke along with the others.

"Look at that!" someone said with surprise. I raised my head. The door of Grandpa Hong's bookstall had been sealed with several *da-zi-bao*. It was too far away to read them. All I could make out were a few words from the titles of the posters: "Propagating Feudal, Capitalistic, and Revisionist Ideals"; "Poisoning our Youth." My mind was full of all the stories I had read there. Now the stories were finished. They were part of the bad system that was going to destroy socialism. I shook my head hard, as if to shake all the evil stories out of my mind.

"Ji-li, come on. Come to school right now. Someone's written a *da-zi-bao* about you. Come on, let's go." An Yi dashed into our apartment, full of alarm. She dragged me to my feet and pulled me to the stairs.

"Wait." I shook off her grasp. "Hold on. What did you say?"

"Your name appeared in a *da-zi-bao*."

I could not believe it. "My name? Why? I'm not a

teacher. Why would they write a *da-zi-bao* about me?"
I could feel my heart race.

"I don't know. But I saw it with my own eyes. Du
Hai and Yin Lan-lan and a couple of others were writing it. I couldn't read it, but I saw your name in the
title." She wheezed heavily and looked at me, wide-
eyed.

We hurried off to the school playground, where the
newest *da-zi-bao* were posted, and searched frantically.
"There it is!" Suddenly I caught sight of it.

The large red characters were like blood on the
poster.

"Let's Look at the Relationship Between Ke Cheng-li
and His Favorite Student, Jiang Ji-li."

I suddenly felt dizzy. Relationship? Me? A relationship with a male teacher? The whole world faded before
my eyes. The only things I could see were the name
Jiang Ji-li and the word *relationship*. A shaft of evening
sunlight flashed on my name. The characters danced
before my eyes, growing larger and redder, almost
swallowing me up.

An Yi was shaking me. Her eyes were full of tears
and she was staring at me anxiously. I could not speak.
I grabbed her arm and we ran out of the school yard.

We stopped at the back door of a small cigarette shop

nearby. An Yi tried to say something, but I wouldn't let her. We leaned against the wall for a long time without saying a word.

"Let's go home." An Yi touched me softly on the elbow. It was getting dark.

"You go ahead. I'm going to read the—" The word "*da-zi-bao*" stuck in my throat.

An Yi nodded worriedly and left.

A half-moon brightened the sky, and the school yard was laced with the ghostly shadows of the parasol trees. I picked my way through the shadows and found the *da-zi-bao* again.

Now, under the cover of darkness, I could let myself cry. I wiped the tears away with my hand, but the more I wiped, the more they came. I pressed my handkerchief to my face. Finally my eyes cleared enough to see.

"Ke Cheng-li doesn't like working-class kids. He only likes rich kids. He made Jiang Ji-li the teacher's assistant for math class and gave her higher grades, and he also let her win all the math contests and awarded her a lot of notebooks. We have to ask the question, What is the relationship between them after all?"

The blood rushed into my head. I felt like throwing up. I leaned against the wall and rested my head on it.

A shadow approached. I tensed and got ready to run. The shadow called out, "Ji-li, it's me. I came back. I was getting worried."

An Yi's voice made the tears gush out of my eyes again. "Oh, An Yi. How could they say these things? How could they say them? A relationship between Teacher Ke and me? It's all lies." My voice was hoarse. "It . . . it . . . it's so unfair. I have never gotten one point, not a single point, that I didn't deserve. And I spent so much time helping Yin Lan-lan and the others with their arithmetic, and now they go and insult me like this. It's disgusting. I—" I could not go on. I bit my handkerchief to hold back my sobs.

An Yi kept silent for a while. She walked beside me with her hand tightly clasping my shoulder. "There were a lot of *da-zi-bao* about my mom, too," she said at last in a soft voice. "They said she was a monster and a class enemy."

I stopped. I was afraid to look at her. Her hand squeezed my shoulder, and I felt her sobbing quietly.

We stood together like that for a long time, in the darkness and the silence.

THE RED SUCCESSORS

When Mom and Dad heard about the *da-zi-bao*, they immediately suggested that I stay home from school for a few days. Since there were no classes, other students were staying home too. Nobody would connect my absence with the *da-zi-bao*.

As it turned out, I came down with a fever and stayed home for ten days.

I lay in bed all day and watched Grandma and Song Po-po work around the house. I was too tired and too depressed to do any more than watch them and watch a patch of sunlight as it moved across the room. As the fever subsided, I began to feel better, but Grandma said I should stay home a few more days to make sure I was completely well. For the first time in my life I was happy to miss school.

Both Song Po-po and Grandma tried their best to cheer me up. Song Po-po combed my hair and made me treats. Grandma sat by my bed, took out my stamp collection, and tried to get me to take an interest in it. Finally, Grandma bought some lovely soft gray wool for me and taught me how to knit a sweater for Dad. I worked on it every day while the others were in school, but slowly, with many pauses, while I stared out the window.

Why would anyone say such terrible things about me? Why did Yin Lan-lan and Du Hai hate me? What had I ever done to hurt them? I asked myself these questions again and again, but I never found an answer.

Every day An Yi came to visit me, sometimes bringing me a bowl of sweet green bean soup from her grandmother. Every day she told me what was happening at school. Classes had started again. They were studying Chairman Mao's latest directives and related documents from the Central Committee. There would be one more month of school before graduation. An Yi said that not many of our classmates had seen the *da-zi-bao* about me. And there were now so many *da-zi-bao*, posted one on top of another, that no one was likely to find mine.

Red Guards were everywhere. Since the newspapers had praised them as the pioneers of the Cultural Revolution, every high school and college had organized Red Guards to rebel against the old system. When the

Central Committee had announced that Red Guards could travel free to other provinces to "establish revolutionary ties" with other Red Guards, An Yi told me, our entire school had gone into an uproar. Most of the students had never been out of Shanghai, so this was terribly exciting news. A large crowd of students from our school had gathered outside the school committee offices and shouted nonstop: "We—want—to be—Red Guards! We—want—to establish—revolutionary ties!" Only college and high school students were allowed to be Red Guards, but our school district had finally granted our school permission to establish the Red Successors. Just as the name indicated, the Red Successors were the next generation of revolutionaries, and when they were old enough, they would become Red Guards. Ten Red Successors were to be elected from each class. An Yi brought me a note from Teacher Gu saying she hoped I was feeling better and would come back to school for the election on Saturday.

Friday afternoon a thunderstorm struck. The darkness gathered until I could not see my book. The first flash of lightning drew me to the window as the downpour began. I sat on a porcelain stool, leaning my forehead against the cool windowpane. The torrent overflowed the gutters, and a curtain of rainwater leaped off the roof. Wind-blown spray blurred the window. The alley was washed clean. Dirt and trash were swept away by the flood. I stared at the downpour and pictured all the *da-zi-bao* in the school yard. I opened the window and shivered with delight as the clean chill air swept over me.

A blast soaked my face and I laughed. From behind me a hand reached out to pull the window shut. Grandma smiled down at me. She knew exactly what I was thinking. She gently wrapped my robe around my shoulders. I lay contentedly in her arms as the rain washed away my humiliation and shame.

By morning the storm had passed.

When we got to school, we found that all the *da-zi-bao* were gone. Sodden fragments littered the school yard, with only a few torn and illegible remnants dangling on the ropes. The paper with my name on it had disappeared. I sighed with relief and went to class feeling better than I had in a long time.

During the time I was home, summer had arrived. The windows of the classroom were all open, and the fragrance from the oleander bushes outside filled the air, heavy, rich, and warm. The classroom itself looked nicer. All the *da-zi-bao* had been taken down and replaced by other things. A big color poster, at least six feet by three feet, hung in the middle of the back wall. It showed a big red flag with Chairman Mao's picture and a long line of people marching under the flag. On the right side of the room, the slogan LONG LIVE THE GREAT PROLETARIAN CULTURAL REVOLUTION covered almost the entire wall. I was cheered by the revolutionary atmosphere.

Teacher Gu walked in, and the election for the Red Successors began.

I lowered my head and pretended to check my nails. I wanted everyone to see that I did not care if I was not chosen. My parents and Grandma had warned me against disappointment, so I was prepared. And anyway, the Red Successors were not nearly as glorious as the Red Guards.

Yu Jian, the chairman of our class, was the first one nominated. Then I heard my name called. My heart raced and I held my breath. I could hardly believe it. I was nominated! After everything that had happened, I was still regarded as somebody in the class! Now I could admit it to myself: I had never wanted anything as much as I wanted to win this election.

I looked gratefully at the student who had nominated me.

Teacher Gu was about to write the names of all the candidates on the blackboard when Yin Lan-lan raised her hand. "When the Red Guards were elected at my sister's school, the class status of the candidates was taken into account. Shouldn't we do the same?"

"Right! Those who don't have good class backgrounds shouldn't be elected," somebody else agreed.

My heart fell. Class status. There was that phrase again.

At a loss for anything to say, I turned around and looked at Yu Jian.

Yu Jian stood up without hesitation. "My class status is office worker. But before Liberation my father used to be an apprentice. He had to work at the shop counter when he was in his teens, and he suffered all kinds of exploitation by the owner. My father is a member of the Communist Party now, and my mother will join pretty soon." All hands were raised to elect him a Red Successor.

It was my turn now. My mind was blank. I did not know what to say. I stood up slowly, the back of my blouse suddenly soaked with sweat.

"My class status is also office worker. My father is an actor. . . ." I stumbled, trying to remember what Yu Jian had said. "He . . . is not a Party member, and neither is my mother. And . . . I don't know what else." I sat down.

"Jiang Ji-li, what is your father's class status?" a loud voice asked.

I slowly stood back up and looked around. Du Hai was staring at me. He sat sideways, one arm resting on the desk behind him.

"My father's class status . . . ?" I did not see what Du Hai meant at first. "You mean what did my grandfather do? I don't know. I only know that he died when my father was seven."

There was a trace of a grin on Du Hai's face. He stood up lazily and faced the class.

"I know what her grandfather was." He paused dramatically, sweeping his eyes across the class. "He was a—LANDLORD."

"Landlord!" The whole class erupted.

"What's more, her father is a—RIGHTIST."

"Rightist!" The class was in pandemonium.

I was numb. Landlord! One of the bloodsuckers who exploited the farmers! The number-one enemies, the worst of the "Five Black Categories," even worse than criminals or counterrevolutionaries! My grandfather? And Dad, a rightist? One of the reactionary intellectuals who attacked the Party and socialism? No, I could not believe it.

"You're lying! You don't know anything!" I retorted.

"Of course I know." Du Hai smirked openly. "My mother is the Neighborhood Party Committee Secretary. She knows everything."

I could say nothing now. Through my tears I could see everyone staring at me. I wished I had never been born. I pushed the desk out of my way and ran out of the classroom.

Outside, it was so bright that I could barely see. Shading my eyes with my hand, I jumped blindly into the dazzling sunshine and ran home.

Grandma was frightened by the tears streaming down my face. "What happened, sweetie? Are you hurt?" She put her spatula down and grasped my hand, asking again and again.

At first I couldn't answer. Finally, still sobbing, I managed to tell her what had happened.

"It isn't true, is it?" I sobbed. "Grandpa wasn't a landlord, was he? Dad isn't a rightist, is he?"

"Of course your father is not a rightist. Don't listen to your classmates," Grandma said immediately, but she sounded nervous.

"And Grandpa wasn't a landlord either, right?" I looked straight into Grandma's eyes.

Grandma heaved a sigh and hugged me to her chest.

"Whatever he was, it doesn't have anything to do with you. He's been dead for over thirty years."

It was true, then. Grandpa was a landlord.

I did not want to listen anymore. I turned away.

When I opened my eyes the next morning, Dad was standing by the bed.

"Get up, Ji-li. I'm taking the three of you for a walk." He patted my cheek.

"I don't feel like going." I rolled over and faced the wall, my eyes swollen and my head heavy and aching.

"You must come. I have something to tell you," he said gently but firmly.

Ji-yong and Ji-yun each took one of Dad's hands, while I listlessly followed. Mom and Dad had spent a long time talking in the bathroom last night, the only place in our home where they could have a private conversation, and I was sure this walk had something to do with what happened to me yesterday.

It was Sunday. The workday streams of people and bicycles were gone, and the street was quiet and peaceful.

We stopped at the China–Soviet Friendship Mansion. The square in front of the mansion was empty except for the white doves, cooing and chasing each other around the fountain.

We sat on the broad steps in front of the entrance. I leaned against a pillar.

Dad came right to the point. "Grandma told me that Ji-li wasn't elected a Red Successor because her classmates asked about our family class status." He turned and looked straight at me.

I bowed my head and fiddled with my red scarf.

"Things like that will probably happen again because of this Cultural Revolution, so I want to tell you something about our family." Dad's voice, like his face, was calm.

He had been born into a large, wealthy family, he told us, with five generations, more than a hundred people, living together in one big compound. The family had once owned vast amounts of land, many businesses, and other kinds of property. By the time Dad was born, most of the money was lost to extravagance and bad luck, and soon the big family was broken up. When Dad was only seven, his father died, and Dad and Grandma lived by themselves. There was not much money left. Dad went to St. John's University in Shanghai on a scholarship, and he tutored some private students to make money, but even so Grandma had to sell some of her jewelry to pay for their daily expenses. When Dad graduated from St. John's in 1949, the Communist Party had just liberated China from Chiang Kai-shek's rule, and Dad was appointed a vice-principal of a primary school.

"This is the true family background," Dad said. "I am not a rightist, and anyone who says I am can go to my work unit and confirm it. As for your Grandpa, he was a businessman and a landlord."

"Dad," Ji-yong asked suddenly, "did Grandpa whip the farmers if they couldn't pay their rent?"

"Or make their daughters be his maids?" Ji-yun added.

Dad looked into their horrified eyes and slowly shook his head. "Grandpa lived in Shanghai all his life and was never in charge of finances. He was already sick when he married Grandma, and he was bedridden until he died eight years later. Of course, I'm not saying that he wasn't guilty. All landlords exploit, and that is certainly a crime. . . ."

"Why did Grandpa want to exploit people?" I interrupted. I just had to know.

Dad looked at me and did not answer. After a moment's silence he took all of us in his arms and said,

"Now listen. What I want you to know is, whether or not your Grandpa was a landlord or an exploiter, *it isn't your responsibility*. Even I don't have a clear memory of him, so it doesn't have to matter to you at all. *You can still hold your heads up.* Understand?"

"But it's still true that because of him I can't be a Red Successor."

"Yes. Your classmates may talk, and our neighbors may talk. We can't help that. You may not be able to join the Red Successors. We can't do anything about that, either. But you don't have to be ashamed, because it isn't your fault. You didn't do anything wrong. Do you see that?"

Looking at Dad's tender eyes, I felt a little better.

In a few weeks I would graduate. I would enter an elite school and study even harder. Maybe I had a bad class status, but I would have good grades. No one could take those away from me.

"It's not my fault," I repeated to myself. "It's not my fault."

The ten Red Successors were elected, Du Hai and Yin Lan-lan among them. Immediately after the election the two of them strutted around with their red armbands prominently displayed, giving orders to the rest of the class. Du Hai squinted more than ever to show that he should be taken seriously. Yin Lan-lan rushed everywhere, with her head up and her chest thrust out proudly. Yang Fan was elected too, and now she echoed everything Du Hai and Yin Lan-lan said. Yu Jian was also part of the group, though his class background was not red. But he seemed uncomfortable following Du Hai and Yin Lan-lan.

I became more quiet and pretended to have no interest at all in their activities.

One afternoon after a class I was hurrying to erase the blackboard. "Come on, Pauper!" I called to my partner, Deng Yi-yi. It was our turn to be classroom assistants. "We'll be late getting the tools for Handicrafts."

"Hey! Don't call people by nicknames!" someone barked. I turned around. Yang Fan was standing in the doorway right behind me.

"Oh, I'm sorry. I forgot. I promise I'll never call you that again," I told Deng Yi-yi with an apologetic smile.

Yang Fan gave a haughty sneer but seemed content with my response.

"It isn't simply a matter of calling people by nicknames. It's a matter of your looking down on working-class people." Yin Lan-lan and two other Red Successors appeared in the doorway behind Yang Fan, all wearing stern expressions. The classroom was suddenly dead quiet.

"Deng Yi-yi is from a poor family and she isn't neatly dressed, so you look down on her and call her Pauper. This is connected with your class standing, Jiang Ji-li. You should reflect on your class origin and thoroughly remold your ideology."

"It wasn't I who gave her that nickname. Everybody calls her that! And I already apologized." I struggled to control my anger.

"What other people do is a totally different question," said Ying Lan-lan. "Other people don't have a landlord grandfather and a rightist father. They don't need to remold themselves."

"Shut up! Don't you dare say my father is a rightist! Who says he's a rightist? Why don't you go to my father's work unit and ask them?"

Yin Lan-lan was shocked. I was so confident, she could tell I was not lying. "Well . . . what about your grandfather then?"

"What about him? He died when my father was just seven. I never even saw him. Why do I have to remold myself? What does he have to do with me?"

"What? Your grandfather was a landlord and you don't need to remold yourself?" Raising her voice and waving her arm with the new Red Successor armband, she screamed almost hysterically to the whole classroom, "Hey, listen everybody! Jiang Ji-li just said that she had nothing to do with her landlord grandfather and she doesn't need to remold herself! She's denying the existence of class struggle!"

She turned back to me, still shouting. "Chairman Mao said, 'In a class society everyone is a member of a particular class, and every kind of thinking, without exception, is stamped with the brand of a particular class.' There is no doubt that your grandfather's reactionary class standing had a bad influence on your father's thoughts, and he naturally passed them on to you. And your grandmother is a landlord's wife. She tells everybody how much she loves you, and she must have a bad influence on you too. And you say you don't need to remold yourself?"

A large crowd was watching from the doorway. I opened my mouth, but no words would come out. The bell rang to begin class. Du Hai, who had been watching the whole time, suddenly announced, "Jiang Ji-li, stay after school. We Red Successors want to talk with you."

"Uh-oh," I heard someone say.

For the next two periods I did not hear anything the teacher said. The terrible words "landlord" and "class standing," Yin Lan-lan's cold face, Du Hai's sly, squinty eyes, spun in my mind. I had always been a school leader, a role model. How could I have suddenly become so bad that I needed to be remolded thoroughly? I had never even met my grandfather. My head ached, and I pressed my fingers hard on my temples.

I walked into the gym. Yu Jian stood by the parallel bars, discussing something with Yang Fan and Yin Lan-lan, who were sitting on the balance beam. Du Hai was beside them, bending over and writing something. Several other Red Successors leaned over his shoulder. When they saw me, they all stopped. Everybody looked at me seriously but hesitantly, as if they did not know how to start.

"Jiang Ji-li," said Du Hai at last, in long, drawn-out tones, "the purpose of our talk today is to point out your problems." He tilted his head slightly, trying to seem very experienced.

I suddenly remembered one day when he had had to stand in the front of the classroom. He was being punished for tying a piece of paper to a cat's tail and setting it on fire.

"Your problems are very serious, you know. For instance . . ." He looked at the paper in his hand. "You and your grandmother often take a pedicab, which reveals your extravagant bourgeois lifestyle. And your family has a housekeeper. That's definitely exploitation. And you never do any housework—"

"Yes, we sometimes take a pedicab instead of a bus, but only when someone is sick and has to see the doctor." Timidly, I tried to explain. "And I've had several talks with my mother about Song Po-po, but she said that Song Po-po doesn't have any other job, so she needs to work for us."

"Shut up!" Yin Lan-lan cut me off with a ruthless wave of her hand. "Today *we* are going to talk to *you*, not the other way round. Nobody asked you to talk. So just listen. Understand?"

I went numb. I stared at her, unable to hear another word. Was this the person I knew? I had helped Yin Lan-lan with her math three times a week for years, explaining each problem to her over and over until she got it right. And Yang Fan. My friends and I had carried her on our backs to and from school for three months when she had broken her leg two years ago. And all of them. What had I ever done to them? Why were they suddenly treating me like an enemy?

One after another they continued to criticize me. I stared at their moving lips, understanding nothing.

Was it my fault that my family was a little better off than theirs? Many a time I had wished that my parents were workers in a textile mill and that we were poor. I had always begged Mom to let me wear patched pants. I had insisted on washing my own clothes even though we had a housekeeper. When my class did collective labor every week, I always volunteered for the heaviest jobs. Hadn't Du Hai and Yin Lan-lan ever noticed that? Suddenly I wished that I had been born into a different family. I hated Grandpa for being a landlord.

"Why won't you answer?" Yin Lan-lan jumped up from the balance beam and roared at me.

"What?" I looked timidly into the enraged circle of faces in front of me.

The Red Successors exploded.

"You weren't even listening, were you?" shouted Yin Lan-lan. "I tell you, Jiang Ji-li, you'd better stop thinking you're the *da-dui-zhang*. It's the Cultural Revolution now, and there are no *da-dui-zhang*s anymore. You're not the chair of anything now."

"It's different now. The teachers won't be protecting you anymore."

"No wonder you didn't write any *da-zi-bao* criticizing the teachers. You have serious problems with your class standing."

"Your grandfather was a big landlord, and you'd better watch out. We won't put up with any of your landlord tricks."

It was so unfair. I was being punished for something I had not done. "No tears. Not now," I told myself, but I could not hold them back. I started to cry.

The Red Successors did not know what to do. They looked at one another and did not say anything. After a minute Du Hai said in a softer voice, "You can go home now. We'll talk later. You'd better think seriously about your problems."

I walked out of the gym, my mind made up. We were going to graduate in a few weeks, and I would never speak another word to any of them.

Alone in the corner of the school yard I saw a little wildflower. She had six delicate petals, each as big as the nail of my little finger. They were white at the center and shaded blue at the edges.

She was as lonely as I was.

I did not know her name. Softly I stroked her petals, thinking that I would take care of her, as I wished someone would take care of me.

GRADUATION

Teacher Gu announced the latest revolutionary reform of the educational system. The junior high school entrance examination had been abolished. There would be no final exams for us this year. Everyone would automatically graduate.

"Hurray!" An Yi turned around in her seat and beamed at me. "The summer is ours!"

The junior high school entrance examination dreaded by all of us was gone. What a relief! We would not have to spend the whole summer studying for the exam and worrying about what school we would get into. We could play.

Du Hai sat on his desk roaring with laughter. To him, and to Yin Lan-lan, and to the others who were not even sure of graduating, this was wonderful news.

But as I watched Du Hai, my elation suddenly evaporated. Yes, I would have a whole summer to play. But without an entrance exam, how would they pick the students for the elite schools? Ever since third grade I had been counting on getting into Shi-yi, one of the best junior high schools in Shanghai. Then I had planned on attending an elite high school, and then one of the famous universities. Without an entrance exam, how could I be sure of getting into Shi-yi? What could I do to make up for my family background?

While the others were laughing and shouting with delight, I mourned.

An Yi had an asthma attack and was out of school for a week. I went to school and went home by myself. I spoke to almost no one. I kept away from the Red Successors, from the rest of my classmates, from everyone.

"Good morning, Teacher Gu."

I met her in the hallway, but I tried to avoid any more than a polite greeting.

"Ji-li, wait a minute." She would not let me go.

I avoided her eyes as I waited for her to speak.

Teacher Gu had been our homeroom teacher for two years. In those two years she had been more than a teacher to us; she had been a devoted friend. I knew that she had a daughter just my age, and I often felt she was like a mother to me, too.

Before the Cultural Revolution she had been a Model Teacher. Now she was the subject of many *da-zi-bao* calling her an opportunist, a black executioner, a corruptor of the young. Even though I did not believe these accusations, I did not want to be seen with her. I did not want to give the Red Successors another excuse to attack me. Besides, I was ashamed of my own black background. For nearly a month I had tried to avoid her.

"Ji-li, don't be so unhappy."

"I'm not unhappy," I tried to say, but when my eyes met hers, my voice broke. I turned away. I did not know how to face her after all my recent humiliations.

"I have some good news for you." She gently turned my face toward her.

My eyes darted down the hall to make sure no Red Successor saw us together.

"You know the junior high school admissions policy has been changed," Teacher Gu said. "Instead of an entrance exam, teachers are assigning students to their schools." She paused. "Ji-li, all the sixth-grade teachers agreed to assign you to Shi-yi Junior High."

"Shi-yi . . . ?" My dream! In spite of everything it was coming true!

"That's right," she said. "You looked like you

needed some good news to cheer you up." She patted me on the head and turned toward the office building.

I could not move as I watched her walk away. Shi-yi! Even though I could not be a Red Successor, I would go to Shi-yi! I saw the badge of Shi-yi Junior High sparkling on my blouse. I had almost given up, but my teachers had not. The lonely flower had not been forgotten after all. I was happier than I had been for weeks.

Then I felt myself blush. I had tried to avoid Teacher Gu. I had not wanted anyone to see me talking to her. I had not supported her as she had supported me.

"Teacher Gu!" I called after her. "Thank you!" She turned and smiled at me, and I thought of something else. "Teacher Gu, what school was An Yi assigned to?" Seeing her hesitate I added, "She's been sick. She needs some good news too."

"The same as you. Don't tell anyone, okay?"

I ran all the way to An Yi's house. People turned to look at me as I raced by, but I could not stop grinning. I would always work hard, I told myself. I would never let my teachers down.

We graduated.

We had no graduation ceremony, and no party. With so much happening, it seemed that no one had time for such things. An Yi and I were disappointed, but thinking about Shi-yi made us happy again. We decided that we could not wait until fall to get our new school supplies, and so one day we went shopping for them.

We threaded our way through the crowd at the Number One Department Store, searching the store for just the right green schoolbag, large enough to carry ten big books. At the stationery counter we carefully chose new pencil boxes. An Yi's had two long-legged cranes on the cover. Mine had a range of snowy mountains. Our new lunch boxes were the kind we had always dreamed of: bright aluminum with two removable trays, one for rice and one for a meat or vegetable dish. They were real grown-up lunch boxes, proof that we had risen to the status we had looked forward to for so long.

We did not take the bus back home. We walked instead, so that people would see us carrying our perfect new schoolbags and our dazzling new lunch boxes. We were sure that everyone we passed on the street knew that we were going to attend one of the city's best schools.

No longer crowded with students, Xin Er Primary School seemed much larger and quieter during summer vacation. A bird calling from a parasol tree sounded shockingly loud, and our footsteps echoed in the empty hallway.

Less than a week after we had bought our new lunch boxes, An Yi and I had heard a rumor from some of our classmates. They said that the teachers' assignments had been canceled. We could not believe this was true, but we were anxious. We decided to visit Teacher Gu's office and ask her ourselves.

We tapped on the door and she let us in.

The small office had changed. Beautiful calligraphy scrolls had been replaced by a poster of Chairman Mao, and the knickknacks in the bookcase were gone.

Teacher Gu looked at us expectantly. Even though we had been waiting all week to see her, now that the moment had come, it was hard to ask the question.

"We heard that teachers can't assign students to the schools after all. We just wondered . . ." My voice trailed off.

Teacher Gu nodded. "We got a new directive from the city. All students will be assigned to schools by their residential districts. The teachers' assignments have been invalidated."

"Invalidated . . ." I murmured. Another beautiful dream gone. I had been counting the days before the new term began. Now I saw the Shi-yi badge flash before my eyes and disappear. So did the new lunch box. They were gone in an instant, like soap bubbles.

"Does that mean that everyone from the same neighborhood will go to the same school?" I whispered.

"That's right. Everyone from your neighborhood will be in Xin-zha Junior High School."

"And Du Hai and Yin Lan-lan too?"

Teacher Gu stood up and put her arms around us. "Don't worry," she said softly. "Things are bound to change for the better. They will. Cheer up. It will be all right."

An Yi and I came out of the office and stood in the hallway for a long while. We turned to leave.

"Let's take one more look at the school," I suggested. We walked to our old classroom.

The cut-paper characters STUDY HARD AND ADVANCE EVERY DAY still hung on the front wall, but several pins were missing and some of the characters hung askew. The neatly designed and decorated Students' Garden was written over with crude letters that read REVOLUTIONARY ACTIONS.

I sat at my desk, which now felt small and slightly unfamiliar. Once more I looked at the sword carved into the top long ago by some naughty boy. As my fingers traced the grooves in the wood, I could hear Teacher Gu's voice saying, "It will be all right." I looked around the room one more time before I left, and Du Hai's jeers seemed almost as far behind me as the day I had been elected *da-dui-zhang*.

We walked past the library. I had spent many hours in that small room and had discovered many of our national heroes there: brave Liu Hu-lan, who died rather than surrender to a Nationalist warlord; heroic Huang Hi-guang, who sacrificed himself to save his comrades in Korea; and others who gave their lives for the revolution. Now there was a sign on the door that said CLOSED FOR SORTING DURING SUMMER VACATION, and I could see that half the shelves were empty. I knew that many of my favorite books, like the stories in Grandpa Hong's bookstall, would be sorted away forever, declared poison under the new standards.

We turned and left the school yard for the last time.

THE SOUND OF DRUMS AND GONGS

The heat of summer had begun in earnest. At noon the sun scorched overhead, and the familiar slow drone of the popsicle man floated in through the open windows, accompanied by the rhythmic clap of a wooden block on a box: "Ice-cold popsicles. Green bean popsicles. Red bean popsicles. Ice-cold popsicles." My hands sweated so much holding the wool that I could not knit. Instead, I worked on embroidering a pillow sham as I waited for the cool of the evening. In the distance I could hear the sound of drums and gongs.

There was a tension in the air that even we children felt. The newspapers and radio were full of the campaign to "Destroy the Four Olds." The campaign had been expanded to eliminate personal possessions. "If we do not completely eliminate the roots, the plant will grow back," we heard. "We must eradicate these relics of the past. . . . We must not allow the reactionary forces to hoard their treasures. . . ." And every day we heard the drums and gongs that meant the Red Guards were ransacking the houses of class enemies to find and confiscate their hoarded possessions.

One day the drums and gongs approached closer than I had ever heard them before. Ji-yun and her classmate Xiao Hong-yin ran into the house, full of the news. "It's a search party, all right," Ji-yun shouted. "They came from Old Man Rong's factory in trucks and they posted a *da-zi-bao*. Come on! Let's go see." She dragged me down the stairs.

A crowd was already gathering at Number Eleven, old Mr. Rong's house. Two dark trucks blocked the entry. The sides of the trucks were covered with red banners that said things like SWEEP AWAY ALL THE REACTIONARY MONSTERS and DESTROY THE FOUR OLDS AND ESTABLISH THE FOUR NEWS. The big iron gate in front of the building was closed, but there was an unusual clamor coming from inside the house. The indistinct shouts of the Red Guards mingled with the furious barking of Mrs. Rong's huge dog. We could only imagine what was going on inside.

A *da-zi-bao* was posted on the gate, and a solemn crowd had gathered around to read it, wiping their faces with handkerchiefs and shading their heads with palm-leaf fans. Du Hai's mother was there along with another Neighborhood Party officer. I pushed my way between the people so I could read the *da-zi-bao*.

"Though the capitalist Rong De-feng has died, his widow still lives on his ill-gotten gains. The factories in which her husband exploited the masses have been returned to their rightful owners, the workers and the People's government. Yet the reactionary monster still lives on the blood of the workers. Instead of admitting her crimes and striving to atone for her sins, Old Lady Rong has sent her sons to Hong Kong, where they can continue to exploit the Chinese people, and she herself continues to flaunt her bourgeois life. The Red Guards have determined to eradicate the roots of this noxious weed in order to promote Chairman Mao's revolutionary cause."

I had never seen a search, except in the movies. I knew that they were the only way we were going to get rid of the Four Olds, once and for all. Still, there was something about the idea that made me nervous.

Ji-yun pulled on my arm. "Ji-li, what does 'noxious' mean?" Before I could answer her, Grandma was at my shoulder.

"Ji-li, help me carry this bag. Ji-yun, come along home now." She hustled us away. Ji-yun was still jabbering excitedly, but Grandma was stern. "You children

stay in the house this afternoon, you hear? That's nothing for you to gawk at."

When Ji-yong came back in, he was thrilled too. He
had spent part of the day in the park and had missed
some of the excitement. "I saw them driving away a
truck just full of stuff. I'm going back to see what else
they got."

"You'll do nothing of the kind," Grandma said
sharply. "Those poor people have enough to worry
about without your going to stare at them." I was not
sure who Grandma was worried about, the Red Guards
or Mrs. Rong, but it was clear that she did not want us
involved.

All that afternoon I was restless. I pictured Mrs.
Rong, sitting under guard, cursing because her fourolds
were being found. I imagined the searchers ransacking
the trunks and drawers and drilling holes in the walls to
look for hidden valuables. It seemed both inspiring and
scary. When Grandma asked me buy her some soy
sauce, I could not help seizing the opportunity to go
past Number Eleven and take another look.

People just getting home from work had swelled
the crowd at the gate. Some of them were clustered in
front of the *da-zi-bao*, but many more were talking in
small groups. Children ran up and down the alley

around and through the knots of people. One boy dared to hit a gong, and the clang startled everyone. The alley fell into silence. Everyone turned to look at the boy, and he scurried to stand behind his father. The conversation continued in hushed tones.

"It's no surprise to me," said a woman I recognized as the housekeeper from Number Nine. "Every day when she went out all dolled up, I said to myself, she is heading for a fall."

"Last New Year's she went out with a new diamond ring bigger than I ever saw before," another old woman said. "Mrs. Feng's housekeeper told me it was over three carats. And the clothes she had made in Hong Kong! Every time somebody else got a new dress, you could be sure Mrs. Rong would get a prettier one."

"Yes, and the taxicabs and the dinners. . . . And mah-jongg all night sometimes."

I moved closer to the *da-zi-bao* on the gate.

"They said she had hundreds of thousands of yuan in the bank."

"I heard a million! My uncle worked in one of his factories before Liberation, and he knew all about Old Rong." This was Mr. Ni, the man we called Six-Fingers because of the extra finger on his right hand. He lived in one of the converted garages in our alley.

"The antiques they carried out a while ago must have been worth a million all by themselves."

"And there was that trunk full of gold bars. They could hardly carry it." There was satisfaction in their voices.

The gate opened with a loud clang and I jumped. Eight men struggled out with a huge mahogany four-poster bed. It was just like Mom and Dad's bed, with a mirror in the headboard surrounded by carved dragons. Most of the crowd murmured in admiration, but I also heard an indignant snort.

"Typical capitalist," said a ragged-looking old woman.

I blushed. Our family had a capitalist bed, too. I turned and made my way out of the crowd.

The sound of drums and gongs drew near again. I saw Grandma wince. "Who is it this time?" she muttered. "You children stay in the house this afternoon." She wearily turned back to the kitchen.

Everyone could identify the sounds of a search, and we had grown expert at locating them in the neighborhood. After six more searches had been conducted in our alley, they were no longer exciting, but the adults I knew grew more and more tense.

Only Ji-yong was still enthusiastic about them. He always seemed to know the latest stories. "The house-keeper at Number Eighteen told the searchers that there were gold bars hidden in the toilet tank," he laughed. "At Number Twenty-seven, where Lu's mistress lives, they found his wife's jewelry." And, most riveting of all, "They found real weapons at Number Thirty-eight." His voice was hushed with excitement. "They went up into the attic and looked in the old chimney, and they found a gun!"

"And do you know what else?" Song Po-po added, really speaking to Grandma rather than to us. "Six-Fingers is always at every search. He's too sick to work at the light bulb factory, but he's not too sick to go to every search and carry things out. He has all the rough-est little children organized into a kind of posse to help keep order. He says he's proud to be doing his part." Grandma raised her head, but I heard no response.

It was hard to imagine where Song Po-po heard so much news. When neighbors ran into each other, they did not stop to chat but just nodded and hurried on. Everyone felt vulnerable, and no one wanted to say anything that would cause trouble. We children were warned to stay close to home and come back at once if a search occurred. Only some of the few working-class people in the alley still seemed excited when they heard the drums and gongs.

In other years summer vacation had been a happy time. In the daytime we went to the pool or to the movies or to the park to turn somersaults and roll on the grass. Evenings we sat in the alley with the neighbors and listened to stories. We would watch the moon and sing and giggle until very late.

Now things were different. An Yi had been sent away to spend the summer with her grandparents in Shandong, away from Shanghai's turbulence. I missed her terribly. I saw hardly any kids in the neighborhood. No one came out to play. There seemed to be no laughter in the alley—just a growing, choking tension.

Things got so bad that Mom and Dad decided to dismiss Song Po-po.

I heard Mom speaking to her in the kitchen. "We really hate to let you go. But if the Red Guards found out, they would accuse us of exploiting working people." Mom's voice sounded uncomfortable. She paused for a moment, then continued, "We want to give you this in thanks. . . ."

That evening Song Po-po carried a small bag downstairs with her. Her eyes were red, and she seemed even more hunchbacked than usual.

I did not know why she seemed so sad. Song Po-po was part of the family, and it was good that she was not working for us. It meant we were not exploiting her.

I thought of everything Song Po-po had done for us. On rainy days she would meet us at the school gate with three pairs of boots in a plastic bag, and two umbrellas under her arm. Often she was half soaked when we got home, but we were always perfectly dry. When we ate up all the sweets Grandma bought us and wanted more, Song Po-po would buy us a popsicle or a sweet roll out of her own limited funds.

Unlike other housekeepers, Song Po-po could read—not only books, but music too. Sometimes when we passed her door, we would see her sitting in her wicker chair with a music book in her hand, humming a folk song from her hometown. Ji-yong and Ji-yun would throw themselves into her lap and try to sing along, while I would stand behind her and play with her naturally curly hair.

My Fourth Aunt once told me that people with naturally curly hair were fated to suffer. That was certainly true in Song Po-po's case. She had come from a wealthy family, but her husband had committed suicide after his business went bankrupt. All their money went to pay his debts, and she had had to become a housekeeper. It was very sad, and when I remembered this, I was even happier we were no longer exploiting her.

She still lived in the small room downstairs. We could still visit her and play with her fascinating hair. But we no longer heard her happy humming, and she no longer bought us treats or met us with umbrellas when it rained.

With Song Po-po gone there was a lot more work for us to do. Excited at the idea of getting up and going out at dawn, I volunteered to buy meat and vegetables at the market. This was the hardest job, but considering Grandma's age—she was over seventy—and Mom's and Dad's busy schedules, I felt it was my duty. It was also a good chance to get rid of my remaining bourgeois habits.

The first few days I was overwhelmed. I couldn't identify some of the vegetables I was supposed to buy. I couldn't tell if the fish was fresh or not. Most of all, facing so many people and so many lines, I was totally lost. Each item had its own line, and everything was first come, first served. Often, after standing in a long line for one vegetable, I found that everything else I needed was sold out. Even items that required ration coupons ran out early. But I learned fast. Soon I knew how to pick the best produce and the freshest fish, how to choose the right lines to buy the best food in the shortest time. I learned to stand in one line while having my place held in another, so I could be sure of getting everything Grandma wanted despite the shortages.

Every morning at five thirty I left the alley. I hurried through the empty streets feeling excited and proud. I was a grown-up now, doing a grown-up's job. I was clearly not one of the pampered bourgeoisie.

One day Grandma got sick, and I took over the cooking as well.

When the old square German clock struck twelve, Ji-yong appeared at my shoulder. "You said lunch would be ready by now," he grumbled.

"Just stop bothering me, will you!" I pushed my sweaty hair off my forehead. The kitchen, located on the landing and crammed with pots and pans and a two-burner gas stove, was crowded and stuffy. With the heat from the sun outside and the heat from the stove in front of me, I was simply melting.

I turned to the instructions Mom had left for me. "Steam the eggs for twenty minutes, then add some soy sauce." I lifted the cover of the wok and gasped in dismay.

Oh, no!

The bowl holding the eggs must have overturned into the boiling water. Now, instead of steamed eggs, I had a pot full of egg soup! I decided to mix the egg soup with the rice (which I had burned earlier) anyway. I poured soy sauce into the whole mess and shouted, "Lunch is ready."

Ji-yong did not seem as hungry as he had been. Ji-yun picked at her plate. Grandma said I did very well, but I noticed she hardly ate anything either. I worried that her arthritis had gotten worse, even though she had been lying down all morning.

"Can I get anything for you, Grandma?" I asked.

"No, I'll be all right. When your mother gets home, I'll have her take me to the clinic for acupuncture. That always helps."

"We can take you to the clinic," Ji-yong said.

I gave him a questioning look.

"The Neighborhood Party Committee has a pedicab in their courtyard," he said. "You can borrow it if someone in your family is sick. I can ride it if you help me get started."

"Sweetie, that's nice of you to offer, but I think you'd better get some experience first," Grandma said.

"I've ridden it lots of times." Ji-yong saw my face, and just as Grandma coughed, he amended softly,

"Well, a few, anyway. To practice."

"Mom won't be home till late," I pondered aloud. "If we help push, and Ji-yong goes slowly, we can do it."

"If you're sure . . ." Grandma said. She must have been in a lot of pain. That decided me.

Ji-yun helped Grandma down the steps while Ji-yong and I got the pedicab. Standing in front of us, it seemed much bigger, much blacker, much less friendly than I remembered. Slowly we pushed it back to our house. Grandma clambered stiffly into the covered seat in back, and we set off.

Ji-yong's legs were too short, so he had to stand up to turn the pedals. Ji-yun and I pushed from behind. The pedicab moved cautiously down the alley and entered the busy street. The traffic light turned red, and the pedicab slowed down as Ji-yong pressed the hand brake. We came to a smooth stop. Ji-yong gave a confident smile, and I began to relax.

The light turned green. Ji-yong stood up on the pedals again, but the pedicab did not move. "Push!" he shouted, and I leaned into the pedicab with all my might. At last it began to move. We had just mastered a slight rise and had reached the middle of an intersection when a bus horn blared in my ear. The light had changed without our realizing it, and the bus driver was waving at us to get out of the way. I gave a start and nearly fell, just as Ji-yong picked up some speed. By the time I recovered, the pedicab was ten yards in front of me and gaining. Ji-yun had stopped when she saw me slip. Now we both ran after the pedicab.

Ahead of us Ji-yong turned back to smile at Grandma, and the pedicab swerved crazily toward the curb. I shouted. Ji-yong turned back and yanked on the handlebars. One back wheel jolted up over the sidewalk and back down to the street. Ji-yong did not slow down. We finally caught up to them at the next red light.

As we panted up to the pedicab, the light changed. "Push!" Ji-yong shouted over his shoulder.

I shook my head. "You'd better slow down. You nearly made Grandma fall out when you hit that curb." I looked into the pedicab and saw Grandma kneading her hands nervously. "Ji-yong has already promised me to be more careful," she said with a stern glance at his back. From his sheepish smile I knew that she had given him a real scolding.

All the rest of the way to the clinic, and all the way home again, we drove slowly and carefully. Even Ji-yong gave a sigh of relief when we were back in the alley at last.

But I heard him boast to Mom when she got home

from work. "It was easy," he said. "Anytime Grandma needs to go to the clinic, we'll just take her."

Dad was often kept late at the theater, and sometimes he did not come home until after we were in bed. There were a lot of meetings, he told us. Often I would wake up when I heard him come in, and as I went back to sleep, I heard him and Mom talking in low voices. They must have made their decision about the trunks at one of those late-night conferences, but the first we knew about it was on a Sunday morning when they started carrying the trunks up to the roof.

The four trunks were part of Grandma's dowry. They were a rich red leather, with a pattern stamped in gold. Each trunk had two sets of brass locks on its front and a round brass handle on each end. When they were stacked up on their rack, they made our room shine. Now Dad was going to dye them black so that they would not be considered fourolds.

Four stools were waiting in the middle of the roof, and the first chest was placed upon them. The dark dye was already mixed. Dad set to work.

"Wait a minute," exclaimed Grandma. There was a dark stain about the size of a thumb print on one of the brass handles. She took out her handkerchief and rubbed the handle over and over until it was clean and bright. She looked at the chest with a dreamy expression and gently laid her hand on it. Against the deep red leather her skin seemed even paler.

"It won't look bad after it's painted," Dad said softly.

Grandma seemed to wake up. "Oh, I know," she said. "You go ahead." She went down to the room and did not come back.

"Her mother gave her these trunks when Grandma got married. That's why she's sad," Dad explained.

I thought of Grandma getting married so long ago, bringing the four beautiful trunks full of gifts her mother had sent from Tianjin to Shanghai. Grandma must have been excited and exhausted, traveling a thousand miles to marry a man she had never met.

Dad started to paint, wielding the brush awkwardly.

"Dad, it's too dry. Look how it's streaking."

Dad dipped the brush in the dye again.

"Look out! It's dripping, Dad."

Shouting advice, we ran around the trunks excitedly.

Eventually Dad's painting improved, and the first trunk was finished. But the original color could still be seen through the dye, and he had to put on a second coat. Ji-yun and I grew tired of watching and went back downstairs. Ji-yong stayed to help.

An amazing sight stopped the two of us in the doorway.

"Wow," Ji-yun said.

Glowing silks and satins spilled out of an old trunk. The whole room was alive with color.

Ji-yun grabbed a piece of silk. "Gorgeous! Are these costumes, Mom?"

They were old clothes, long gowns like the ones ancient courtiers and scholars wore in the movies. Many of them were embroidered with golden dragons or phoenixes. Some were printed with magnificent colorful patterns, and some were even crusted with pearls and gold sequins.

"These belonged to our ancestors. Grandma thought they were too nice to throw away, so we kept them in the bottom of this chest." Mom reached in and pulled out a bunch of colorful silk neckties. She threw them all on the floor.

I was worried. "Mom, aren't these all fourolds?"

"That's right. That's why Grandma and I decided to make comforter covers out of them. We can use the ties to make a mop."

"It seems terrible to just cut them all up. Why don't we just give them to the theater or to the Red Guards?"

Ji-yun held a gown up in front of her. She was imagining what it would be like to wear it, I knew.

"The theater doesn't need them, and it's too late to turn them in now. The Red Guards would say that we were hiding them and waiting for New China to fall. Besides, even if we did turn them in, the Red Guards would just burn them anyway." Grandma looked at me and shook her head as she picked up her scissors. "I just couldn't bear to sell them," she said sadly. "Even when your father was in college and we needed money." She picked up a lovely gold-patterned robe and said softly, "This was a government official's uniform. I remember my grandfather wearing it."

"It *is* pretty, Grandma," I said, "but it is fourolds. Don't feel bad about it."

The long gowns were so large that the back of one was big enough for half a quilt cover. Mom and Grandma discussed the job while cutting: which parts could be used for covers and which parts for cushions. Ji-yun and I were enchanted by the pearls and gold sequins littering the floor. We pestered Grandma and Mom to let us have them, and finally Mom sighed and yielded.

Ji-yun and I were overjoyed. We sat amid the piles of silks, picking up pearls and putting them in a jar.

Little White was happy too. She rolled over and over among the scraps of silk and batted pearls around the floor.

While we played, Mom made two quilt covers out of the gowns, one deep purple and the other a bright gold. Then she made a pair of mops from the ties. We were delighted with them. You could not find anything like our tie mops in the stores.

Dad and Ji-yong finally finished the second coat of dye on the trunks. The gold stamping still obstinately showed through the layers, but the deep red had become a dark burgundy. The room seemed dressed up with the glowing new quilts and the repainted trunks. I felt good. We had really done what Chairman Mao asked, breaking with the old and establishing the new.

"You did a nice job on the trunks," Grandma said. "I don't think the Red Guards will notice them."

Ji-yun looked up from the bed where she was lying with her face in the silky new cover. "Are the Red Guards going to come and search our house?"

Everyone stood still. I stopped playing with the pearls. Even Little White stopped rolling around the floor.

"It's possible," Mom said slowly, "but you don't have to be afraid. You are just children, and a search would have nothing to do with you."

The new decor lost all its brightness. The pearls I had been playing with lost their luster, and I put them down.

THE PROPAGANDA WALL

Right at the entrance to our alley, where you could not help noticing it, stood the propaganda wall. It was tall and wide, covering the whole end of one building and looming over the street. Every time a new campaign started, a picture would be painted on it to promote the campaign's message. When I was little, the wall had been covered with a picture of a woman dressed in a cook's white uniform and white hat, and holding a large tray of food. The slogan beneath the picture had been ALL FOR ONE AND ONE FOR ALL. That was when the government was encouraging families to eat at neighborhood canteens to reduce housework and allow women to work outside the family. Right before the Cultural Revolution, the picture had been of a huge mushroom cloud from an atomic explosion, with a tiny big-nosed American trembling in the corner. MASTER NUCLEAR WEAPONS, SCARE THE AMERICAN BARBARIANS, the slogan said.

Now the wall was being painted again. After a few

weeks a beautiful copy of the popular painting *Mao Ze-dong on His Way to Anyuan* appeared in our alley. I had always loved this painting and the story behind it. When he was a young man, our beloved leader, Chairman Mao, had risked his life to go to the mines of Anyuan by himself to establish a revolutionary base there.

The young Mao in the painting wore a long cotton gown and cloth shoes, and he carried an umbrella under his arm. His brilliant eyes were looking into the distance as if he were already thinking about the great revolutionary task that lay ahead of him. I could not look at the painting without feeling inspired. I was ready to follow him anywhere.

As soon as the painting was finished, two new rituals, Morning Repentance and Evening Report, began. Now every morning as I returned from the market in the cool morning air, I saw a group at the foot of the propaganda wall. Five or six people who had been landlords or counterrevolutionaries or rightists—people in the Five Black Categories—bowed in front of Chairman Mao. They waved their copies of the *Selected Quotations from the Writings of Chairman Mao*, the Precious Red Book, in the air and chanted, "Long life to Chairman Mao! Long life! Long life! Long life!"

Then one by one they confessed their guilt. In the evening they had to do it again. To my shame Aunt Xi-wen was among them. Like all of them she wore ragged and faded clothes and looked anxious. Six-Fingers, the chairman of the new Neighborhood Dictatorship Group, presided over them, wearing a red armband and an expression of importance.

I could not help watching as the Five Black Categories confessed. But when they bowed their heads before the picture, they did not look sorry to me so much as weary. Or perhaps sullen or resigned. I could never decide what it was they seemed to feel.

If I came back a little later, Aunt Xi-wen and the others would be at work sweeping their assigned parts of the alley. After the first few days Six-Fingers would not let the boys throw stones at them, but the boys still gathered to jeer and taunt the sweepers. With lowered faces the sweepers swept on. They did not raise their heads, not even when Six-Fingers strutted by to stand over them and check their work. When every scrap of paper in the street had disappeared, they shuffled home, heads still bowed.

The Neighborhood Dictatorship Group and the Black Categories were all we could think of. Neighbors discussed who was in each group and wondered what would happen next. More and more, Six-Fingers and the rest of the Neighborhood Dictatorship Group seemed to be everywhere. They suggested names of possible Black Category families to the Neighborhood Party Committee. They monitored what the members of the Black Categories did during the day, recorded any visitors to their homes, watched their Morning Repentance and Evening Reports, and supervised their sweeping the alley twice a day. In addition, the Neighborhood Dictatorship Group patrolled the neighborhood day and night. As chairman of the group, Six-Fingers was especially cocky and especially visible.

One evening they actually caught a counterrevolutionary! A ragpicker, who was collecting scrap paper to recycle, pulled some old *da-zi-bao* off the wall and happened to tear the newspaper that was posted underneath. A picture of Chairman Mao on this newspaper ripped in half. Witnessing this criminal act, Six-Fingers and his deputies immediately detained the man and took him to the police station.

After that, Six-Fingers was cockier than ever.

The notice posted next to the propaganda wall drew everyone's attention. Jia Hong-yu, our district's most famous Red Guard leader, had returned from Beijing and would give her report at a neighborhood meeting.

Jia Hong-yu was famous all over the district because she had led a group of Red Guards on a fifteen-day march into the countryside to spread word about the Cultural Revolution, and none of the boys had been able to outwalk her. She also persuaded a spy sent by the Nationalists in Taiwan to confess—without even beating him, although she said she was perfectly willing to beat those who did not confess.

Ji-yong and I had arrived early, but we still ended up sitting near the back of the factory cafeteria. The lazily turning ceiling fans did little to cool the heavy air, and several people around us were smoking, but we hardly noticed. All we could see was Jia Hong-yu.

She was standing on a low stage under a red banner: CHAIRMAN MAO AND THE RED GUARDS—THEIR HEARTS ARE ONE. She wore the belted army uniform and red armband of the Red Guards. In the dim light it was hard to see her face, but it was easy to know how she felt from her voice.

"When Chairman Mao invited the Red Guards to travel to establish revolutionary ties, my father forbade me to go," she began. "My mother was sick and I was needed at home. But how can we put personal matters ahead of the revolution? I saw that it was adopting an individualist line to stay for such a reason, so I secretly packed up my bedroll and left without telling anyone. I determined that I should go to Beijing so that I could establish revolutionary ties, not just with comrades from Beijing, but with comrades from all over China who would meet in Beijing.

"The train was very full. I could not even get in the door, but I refused to let small difficulties stand in my way. I asked some Red Guard comrades in the train to reach their arms out to me and help me to climb in the window. I had to sit on the floor, and I was hungry and thirsty. When night came I had to sleep under the seat, but I didn't mind. Getting used to hard conditions is good for revolutionaries. I thought about our Volunteer Army soldiers and how they had to sleep in the snow in Korea."

Sitting on the hard bench in the cafeteria, I pictured her thirty-hour trip to Beijing, the train crowded with enthusiastic Red Guards. Someone in front of me lit a cigarette. As the match flared, I saw Du Hai sitting in rapt attention.

Jia Hong-yu continued: "It was so stirring to arrive in Beijing. The whole city was crowded with revolutionary comrades. All the guest houses were full, and all the university dormitories were full too, so comrades brought quilts and plates from their own homes and opened their offices to us. I shared an office with seventeen girls from all parts of China. We talked about the revolutionary situations in other places. We were so full of revolutionary zeal that we hardly slept at night. We had to walk all the way to the university for our meals. There were too many of us to sit in the cafeteria, so we all had to take our food outside and sit on the ground to eat. We were so happy to be there that we hardly noticed, even when it rained.

"One day we heard that Chairman Mao was going to receive all the Red Guards at Tienanmen Square." There was a sudden catch in her voice when she said his name. "We all went to the square right away, because we didn't know when he would come. We waited all afternoon. When night came, we stayed. There were thousands of comrades in the square, and we spent all night establishing revolutionary ties. Right next to me there was a comrade whose cousin had seen Chairman Mao. It was hard to believe that I would see him too. No one slept a wink. The next morning many more came. The whole square was terribly crowded. There were tens of thousands of us sitting there, most of us dressed in army uniforms and all wearing red armbands. The sky was blue, and the day was very clear. Everywhere you looked were revolutionary comrades. It was a truly magnificent sight.

"We waited and waited, straining our necks to be the first to see him. The sun was so hot. A few female comrades felt faint, but no one wanted to leave. Some comrades brought us water, but we never even thought of eating anything. Finally at five o'clock in the afternoon the people near the gate started cheering. I looked up, and there he was."

Now her voice broke again. Even from the back I could see tears glistening on her cheeks. "He was right in front of me, up on top of the gate, waving to us. I was crying so much that I could hardly see anything else, but I could see him shining in his army uniform. And then, out of all the comrades in the square, he looked at me! He looked straight at me!"

I felt tears welling out of my eyes. "Anyone who sees Chairman Mao is the happiest person in the world," the saying went. That was my secret dream. And here was someone who had done it! I could not help feeling jealous.

Practically everyone in the crowd was weeping too. I had to strain to hear her as she finished.

"... I am very lucky to have had such an experience," she said. "I have resolved to dedicate my whole life to Chairman Mao and the Great Proletarian Cultural

Revolution. I will give every drop of blood in my body to work to liberate all of mankind."

For a moment the whole room was silent. She raised her arm in a salute, and every teary eye was riveted to the red band she wore.

"Long live Chairman Mao!" someone shouted. Someone else stood up to echo him. Then we were all standing up, all shouting. "Long live Chairman Mao! Long, long live Chairman Mao!"

Wiping my eyes, I slowly walked home. With every step I hoped that Chairman Mao would forgive my black class status and let me be a Red Guard too.

All my life I had seen Old Qian coming and going, his head high, his walking stick in his hand. His lips were always tightly shut, and he spoke to no one. No child in the alley would dare to climb into his courtyard to steal his mulberry leaves. Song Po-po said that he had always been stubborn, and since his son-in-law had been executed as a counterrevolutionary, he had become even more obstinate and solitary.

I was not surprised when he became a target of the Red Guards. In fact, I was proud of them for having the nerve to face him.

Ji-yong had been playing with his friends and had

heard the trouble start. Some Red Guards asked to borrow Old Qian's bicycle, and he refused. The Red Guards had been shocked. When they asked to borrow a bicycle from a black family in the name of the Cultural Revolution, they were not used to being refused. The whole neighborhood had heard their swearing and their threats. " . . . You stubborn counterrevolutionary's family member . . . we'll see which is tougher, your damned old bones, or our Proletarian Dictatorship!" When they returned the next afternoon, we were not surprised.

I heard the familiar sound of drums and gongs and looked out the window. About fifteen Red Guards—and Six-Fingers as well—bustled in and out of Qian's gate. I went back to my reading.

A spate of loud but indistinct shouting drew us all out onto the balcony. Several angry Red Guards pushed Old Qian roughly out the door. One of them put a wooden washboard on the sunny ground in front of the propaganda wall. He shouted something in the old man's face and pointed at the washboard.

Old Qian stood very straight, leaning slightly on his cane. He said something, and the Red Guards burst out shouting once more. The old man just shook his head. Suddenly one of the Red Guards jumped forward. He kicked the cane out of Old Qian's hand and savagely pushed him down on his knees onto the sharp ridges of the washboard.

"Oh my heavens," Grandma gasped. She took Ji-yong and Ji-yun back inside. I did not move.

At first Old Qian knelt on the washboard with defiant erectness. His posture showed no sign of the pain he must have felt. Then, slowly, he began to droop. Occasionally he would sense a Red Guard watching and pull himself up, but for longer and longer periods his gray head was bowed. His wife followed some Red Guards back and forth, saying something and gesturing in supplication. They did not even look at her but busily carried things from Old Qian's house to the truck waiting at the door.

After half an hour she went inside the house once more and then returned with an enamel cup. She knelt beside her husband and held the cup to his mouth. He raised his head and took a few grateful sips. As she lowered the cup, a Red Guard turned around and casually kicked it out of her hand. The water glittered in the hot sun.

I felt sick to my stomach. I went back inside. It was all terribly unnecessary. He was so determined, but so wrong. If he had just lent them the bicycle, none of this would have had to happen.

"What's happening?" Grandma asked anxiously. She lay on her bed with a cold towel on her forehead.

"Still the same." I shook my head and said no more.

I tried to sit and read but found myself pacing up and down the room. My knees hurt when I thought about the washboard, and my head felt dizzy when I imagined the sun burning down on him. "Poor man, he might get heatstroke," I murmured to Grandma. But immediately I scolded myself. How could I feel sorry for a counterrevolutionary's family member who refused to support the Red Guards? Still, I could not help going back out to look at him.

His head was drooping feebly now, and his hands were propped on the ground to keep him from collapsing. His wife sat on the ground beside him, wiping her eyes with a handkerchief.

All afternoon I kept going back to the balcony to look. An hour passed, and another hour, and each time I looked he was still there.

Finally, we heard a shout from his wife. We ran to the balcony. Old Qian had fainted. He lay on his side, half over the washboard, with his sunburned face on the ground.

Several Red Guards rushed out of the house. They

looked flustered as they talked among themselves. After a few minutes they picked the old man up and carried him into the house.

They loaded their truck with all the things they had confiscated, including the bicycle that Qian had refused to lend them. I watched them drive slowly away.

The only things left behind at the base of the wall were a walking stick, a washboard, and an enamel cup, lying on its side.

Even early in the morning the day did not seem fresh. The heavy air seemed to slow the working of my mind. My basket of vegetables dragged heavily on my arm. I passed the propaganda wall and could not help glancing at the ground where Old Qian had knelt yesterday. I started down the alley, but a hushed crowd at An Yi's back door drew me reluctantly down the side lane.

People were packed outside the kitchen craning to see into the back courtyard. ". . . jumped out the bathroom window . . ." I heard. ". . . through the awning of the courtyard . . ." ". . . blood . . ."

I looked around in a daze.

"Old Qian kneeling . . ." "afraid she'd be next . . ." The voices continued to buzz around my ears. I found

112

myself at the front of the crowd, staring at the pieces of the shattered awning. I heard An Yi's grandmother's name and shuddered.

An Yi's grandmother had jumped out the window.

My lips trembled and my teeth began to chatter.

Only a few days ago I had visited her to ask her when An Yi would return from Shandong. She had served me green bean soup she had made herself. She had said that she would like to have An Yi and me accompany her to a dentist appointment when it was cooler. "Then I'll buy you some peaches." Her missing front teeth made ch's sound like ts's.

An Yi's grandmother was short and skinny, and she tottered on her bound feet. Her husband had been a wealthy man, a capitalist. He had owned a dye factory, but he had died a long time ago. For as long as I could remember, An Yi's grandmother had lived with her only child—An Yi's mother, Teacher Wei—An Yi's father, and her elder sister, who was blind. An Yi's grandmother took care of them all. I had known her so long that I called her Grandma too.

Grandma and her sister always dressed in black. Sometimes I saw them up on the roof of their apartment, smoking a water pipe and talking together in their funny Ningbo accent. Grandma loved to give us treats. If An

Yi and I teased or bantered while we studied together, Grandma would say, "Don't be naughty, girls. Do your homework, and then Grandma will give you a treat." When we were greedy, we pretended to quarrel, and it always worked. We thought she did not know we did this.

"Is that white stuff her brain?" a boy's shrill voice called as I turned numbly away. I could not bear to hear any more.

Even though she had committed suicide, I went to Grandma's memorial service at the crematorium.

Through the tall window I could see, across the courtyard, the chimney looming high above, steadily emitting black smoke. The dirty white walls, the white carts with white sheets, the white uniforms on the crematorium workers, and the white, expressionless faces of the dead as they were rolled by all combined to produce an oppressive chill. The acrid smoke and its pervasive smell made me sick to my stomach.

An Yi's grandma lay on a cart, silent under the white sheet. Her face was covered. It had been smashed in her fall, and of course they would not make a wax replacement for a suicide.

Suicide was a crime. It was "alienating oneself from

the people," according to what Chairman Mao said. So we were not in one of the private rooms. We wore no mourning bands. We could not play funeral music for Grandma.

A door opened. We heard the sounds of the traditional dirge grow louder, and so did the screams and wails coming from a memorial ceremony in a private room. A cart trundled by, carrying a body draped in white. The hollow rumble of the hard wheels on the concrete floor went around a corner and slowly died away.

An Yi and her parents stood beside the cart where Grandma lay. Their heads were bowed. No one said a word.

Someone stuck his head out an office door and shouted at Teacher Wei, "Five more minutes!" Without waiting for an answer, he slammed the door shut.

An Yi couldn't hold back her sobs and cried out.

Grandma was so dear to her. When An Yi had an asthma attack, Grandma often had to take her to the hospital for oxygen. As An Yi grew, the job became more and more difficult. Grandma often had to stop for a few minutes before she could continue to move down the stairs from their third floor with An Yi on her back. Once, An Yi said, Grandma had to sit on the stairs and scoot down step by step with An Yi on her lap.

I suddenly remembered a day last summer when I had gone into their house and found Grandma, soaked in sweat herself, holding An Yi's long hair off her neck and fanning her.

I dropped my eyes to the floor and heard the slow music of the dirge, louder for a moment, then soft again.

I shut my eyes and pictured Grandma standing on the windowsill, looking down into the courtyard. What was she thinking before she jumped? She must have forgotten about her duties to her country, and her family too. Did she think about her granddaughter rushing back from Shandong for the funeral? Did she remember her blind sister? I wiped at my tears and took a deep breath.

A kind but shockingly cheerful man in a white uniform appeared. "I'm sorry, but I'll have to take her away now. My boss is already on my back about giving you too much time."

An Yi and Teacher Wei both threw themselves on the cart, sobbing bitterly. The man looked around nervously. "You guys better be careful, or they'll say you're allying yourselves with a bad class, with a suicide and all." We heard a door open down the hall. Suddenly the man pulled An Yi off the cart and pushed it away around the corner. An Yi threw her arms around her mother and they both wailed.

We heard the hollow rumble of the cart, and a squeaking wheel going *eek, eek, eek* into the distance.

A SEARCH IN PASSING

It was already past eight o'clock when Dad's colleagues Uncle Tian and his wife, Aunt Wu, came to visit. They had not come for several months, and things were very different now. Mom did not make her famous beef soup, and Grandma did not make steamed buns. They barely greeted us children when they came in. Instead of loud, lively chatter and jovial laughter, their conversation was all hushed whispers. As soon as they mentioned "the current situation," Dad told us to go downstairs to play with my little cousin Hua-hua.

We went reluctantly. Hua-hua was sleepy and did not want to play patty-cake or any of our usual games, but we stayed at my Fourth Aunt's apartment until we heard the footsteps going down the stairs.

It was late. We were getting ready for bed when Dad talked to us.

"Children, tomorrow I want you to go to the park with Grandma. You'll have to take something for lunch."

Grandma's been sick, I thought. Is this so she can rest?

"A picnic!" Ji-yun shouted. "Oh boy!"

"That's right," Dad answered. "A picnic." His voice sounded odd somehow. "You all go and have a good time."

The morning was still relatively cool when we set off for the park, but the sun was bright and it was sure to be hot before long. I carried a book and a bag that rattled with the dishes we had packed for lunch. Ji-yong and Ji-yun skipped ahead and were already running across the grass by the time Grandma and I arrived.

The park was almost empty. A few old men sat on benches playing chess, and in the shady places some old people did *tai-chi* exercises. We strolled around the lawn, and then Grandma picked a shaded bench and pulled out her knitting. "You go ahead and play," she said. "I'll be right here."

"Let's play tag," Ji-yun said excitedly. We had not been to the park in ages, and the three of us raced around the nearly deserted paths having a wonderful time. We were evenly matched. Ji-yun may have been the youngest, but she was very fast.

Grandma called us to lunch. It was hot now. We gladly rested in the shade while she unpacked hard-boiled eggs and made sandwiches for us. We ate and shared a bottle of juice. We laughed about a trip the whole family had taken to another park last spring, when Ji-yong had dropped the knife out of a rowboat so we had to eat our apples without peeling them. Finally Ji-yong and Ji-yun lay down on some benches and went to sleep. I helped Grandma tidy up before sitting down to read my book. Grandma took out her knitting again but did not set to work. Instead she sighed and stared into space. Her face was pale.

I put my hand on her shoulder.

She turned to me and smiled a little. "Don't worry about me. I'm fine. I've just been worrying too much." She took my hand and patted it gently. "Every time I hear drums and gongs, I'm afraid that they're coming to our house. My heart starts racing, and the closer they come, the worse it gets.

"Now, after seeing poor Old Qian kneeling on that washboard, I haven't been able to sleep. As soon as I close my eyes, I see the Red Guards coming in. I couldn't bear it if they made me kneel like that. Or if they beat me. . . ." She smiled sadly. "Your father and Uncle Tian thought this would help me relax. I can sit in the park all day, and then even if the Red Guards come, I'll be safe here."

"But what if the Red Guards are at our house when we get back?"

"Your father thought of that too. Did you see the mop on the balcony? That's our sign. If the Red Guards come, the mop won't be there and I'll know not to go in."

I was intrigued by the idea of secret signs, but I was scared too. I glanced around to see if someone was watching us.

"It's really not much of a solution," Grandma went on. "I can't stay here all night, and I can't even stay in the park every day for months. Really, I just hope that I'll get used to the situation and won't have to come here anymore." She shook her head sadly.

The breeze blew a strand of hair over her ear, and I gently patted it back into place. She had more gray in her hair, I noticed. And more wrinkles on her face.

She doesn't seem like a landlord's wife, I suddenly thought. In the movies the landlord's wife was ugly, cruel, and stupid. Grandma was beautiful, kind, and smart.

I remembered coming home from kindergarten and showing Grandma the songs and dances we had learned. Grandma sat before us with her knitting, nodding her head in time to the music. Sometimes we insisted that she sing with us, and she would join in with an unsteady pitch and heavy Tianjin accent, wagging her head and moving her arms just as we did.

When we tired of singing, we would pester Grandma to show us her feet. When she was young it was the custom to tightly bind girls' feet in bandages to make them as small as possible—sometimes as small as three inches long. This was considered the height of a woman's beauty. Grandma's feet were half bound, and when she was only seven she fought to have them released. As a result her feet were smaller than natural feet but larger than bound ones. We loved to touch them and play with them. If she refused to let us, we would tickle her until she panted with laughter.

All my friends loved coming to our home because she was so friendly. She had lived in our alley for over thirty years without a single disagreement with any of the neighbors. Everyone loved her and respected her.

Dad had said that she had never been classified as a landlord's wife. She couldn't be, I told myself.

Mom got home from work that evening looking nervous. She whispered to Dad and Grandma, and as soon as we finished dinner, she told us to go outside and play.

"We have something to take care of," she said. I knew this had something to do with the Cultural

Revolution. I wished she would just say so. We were too old to be fooled like little children. But I didn't say anything and went outside with the others.

When it was nearly dark, Ji-yun and I went back home, leaving Ji-yong with his friends.

As we entered the apartment, I smelled smoke, acrid and choking. I looked around in alarm. But Grandma was sitting alone in the main room, showing no sign of worry.

"Grandma, is there a fire?" we shouted anxiously. "Don't you smell the smoke?"

"Hush, hush!" Grandma pulled us to her quickly. "It's nothing. They're just burning some pictures." We looked puzzled. "Your mother heard today that photos of people in old-fashioned long gowns and mandarin jackets are considered fourolds. So your parents are burning them in the bathroom."

"Can we go watch?" I loved looking at pictures, especially pictures of all those uncles and aunts I had never met.

Grandma shook her head. I winked at Ji-yun, and we both threw ourselves into her arms, begging and pleading. As always, she gave in, and went to the bath-room door to ask Mom and Dad.

Mom opened the door a crack and let us in.

The bathroom was filled with thick smoke that burned our eyes and made us cough. Dad passed us a glass of water. "We can't open the window any wider," he said. "The neighbors might notice the smoke and report us."

Mom and Dad were sitting on small wooden stools. On the floor was a tin washbowl full of ashes and a few pictures disappearing into flames. At Dad's side was a stack of old photo albums, their black covers stained and faded with age. Dad was looking through the albums, page by page, tearing out any pictures that might be fourolds. He put them in a pile next to Mom, who put them into the fire.

I picked up one of the pictures. It was of Dad, sitting on a camel, when he was about six or seven years old. He was wearing a wool hat and pants with suspenders, and he was laughing. Grandma, looking very young and beautiful and wearing a fur coat, was standing beside him.

"Mom, this one doesn't have long gowns or anything," Ji-yun said. "Can't we keep it?"

"The Red Guards might say that only a rich child could ride a camel. And besides, Grandma's wearing a fur coat." She threw it into the fire.

Mom was right, I thought. A picture like that was fourolds.

The flames licked around the edges of the picture.

The corners curled up, then turned brown. The brown spread quickly toward the center, swallowing Grandma, then the camel, and finally Dad's woolen hat.

Picture after picture was thrown into the fire. Each in turn curled, melted, and disappeared. The ashes in the washbowl grew deeper. Finally there were no more pictures left. Mom poured the ashes into the toilet and flushed them away.

That night I dreamed that the house was on fire.

By the third day Ji-yong and Ji-yun had tired of spending their days in the park, so they stayed home with our Fourth Aunt. I was bored too, but I wanted to keep Grandma company. So I brought a book and bought a pomegranate. Pomegranates had so many seeds that they took a good long time to eat, and I had plenty of time to spare.

I sat on our usual bench, prying the juicy red seeds out of the fruit and slowly sucking on them one by one, staring at the fleecy white clouds. One cloud looked like a two-humped camel, and another looked like an old man whose long, white beard nearly reached the ground. The camel was leading the old man slowly past.

Grandma coughed and I looked at her, but she was staring into the distance.

In the three months since the Cultural Revolution had started, changes had been so constant that I often felt lost. One day the Conservative faction were revolutionaries that defended Chairman Mao's ideas; the next day, the opposite Rebel faction became the heroes of the Cultural Revolution. I heard that even Chairman of the Nation Liu Shao-qi and General Secretary Deng Xiao-ping were having problems. No one knew what would happen tomorrow.

I wondered what I would be doing if I had been born into a red family instead of a black one. Searching people's houses? Hating landlords and rightists? Of course I would hate them; I hated them even now. I hated my grandfather, just as I hated all of Chairman Mao's enemies. But I had felt sorry for Old Qian even though he was wrong. And I did not know if I could hate Grandma if she was officially classified as a landlord's wife. The harder I tried to figure things out, the more confused I felt. I wished I had been born into a red family so I could do my revolutionary duties without worrying.

When we got home, the mop was still hanging from the balcony.

A week had passed, and still nothing had happened. I waited anxiously, not knowing what I waited for.

It was late in the afternoon.

"Ji-yong's been fighting again," Ji-yun announced as soon as she saw him walk in. His T-shirt was covered with dirt, and one sleeve was half torn off. He carried a broken-strapped sandal.

"What happened?" Grandma rushed in from the kitchen.

"They robbed me! They took my army cap." He wiped his face with his sleeve and angrily threw his sandal on the floor.

"Robbed you? You must have done something to upset them," I scolded. "Why would anybody just grab your cap for no reason? You shouldn't be so ornery to people. Don't go making more trouble for us."

"How can you say that? I was just minding my own business, looking for crickets. They wanted to trade a cricket for my cap, and when I said no, they just took it."

"Who were they? Do you know them?"

Ji-yong nodded grimly. "They won't get away with this, I swear!"

The army cap was one of Ji-yong's treasures. It wasn't one of the ordinary olive-green caps you could buy in a store. It was a real army cap that he had gotten from his friend Ming-ming's father, a Liberation Army veteran. It had been washed and sun bleached until it was nearly white, and anybody could see at a glance that it was the real thing. All the boys envied his cap. No wonder he was so angry.

"Well, it's only a hat. Forget about it. It's not worth stirring up trouble." Grandma took out her sewing kit to mend his shirt.

"Just wait, I'll get it back," he said, more to himself than to us. "Chairman Mao didn't say that I can't wear an army cap."

I turned to him attentively. "What do you mean? Who said that you couldn't?"

"They said it. They said, 'What's a black whelp like you doing with a real army cap?'" His eyes flashed with anger.

Now I understood. Calling him a black whelp was the real cause of the incident.

Of course a boy like Ji-yong would rather fight than take an insult like that. I wished I could protect him, but there was nothing I could do. I suddenly remembered that An Yi's uncle used to be a mechanic in the army. Maybe he would still have an old cap. I decided to ask An Yi about it.

In a little while Ji-yong disappeared. I was sure he had gone to find his buddies, Xiao-cheng and Ming-ming.

Xiao-cheng and Ming-ming were our neighbors. Despite the fact that they were both three years older than Ji-yong and all three of them attended different schools, the three boys were close friends. In our alley they were known as "the three musketeers" because they were always together.

Xiao-cheng's father had been our District Superintendent. Now he was suspended and under investigation for being a capitalist follower. Ming-ming's father had been the Party Secretary of the Shanghai Institute of Political Science and Law, and had been under arrest at the Institute for several weeks. He had been accused of being a traitor.

Their family problems drew the three black whelps together more than ever.

The next afternoon when Grandma and I came back from the park, Ji-yong was not at home. He was not home at dinnertime, either. I went to Xiao-cheng's and Ming-ming's houses, but none of the boys were there.

"Where did he go?" Grandma scolded. "How could he miss dinner?"

I was worried. I was sure that he and his friends had gone to get the cap back. I should have mentioned An Yi's uncle, I thought, but I knew it would not have made any difference. If Ji-yong decided to do something, nothing I said would stop him. He was going to get hurt, and probably get the family in more trouble.

At eight thirty he came in. He had a black eye, and he was limping, but he had a smile on his face.

"Were you fighting again?" Mom snapped. "Don't you think we have enough to worry about without you fighting too?"

"We got my cap back!" He raised it triumphantly.

"Look, the brim's been torn off." Ji-yun snatched the cap out of his hand.

"You got a black eye for a rag like this?" I asked.

"It was worth it," he said. "They won't dare push me around anymore."

I bit back the scolding I wanted to give him and got him a cold towel for his eye.

Early in the morning Song Po-po rushed upstairs to tell us the news. All the neighbors were saying that a knife had been found in the communal garbage bin. The Neighborhood Dictatorship Group had declared this to be an illegal weapon, so the entire bin had been searched and some incompletely burned pictures found. In one of them they recognized my Fourth Aunt. Because my Fourth Uncle had fled to Hong Kong right before Liberation, her family was on the Neighborhood Party

Committee's list of black families. The weapon was automatically associated with the pictures, and that was enough for Six-Fingers to report to the powerful Neighborhood Party Committee.

All day we were terrified. Grandma and the three of us went to the park immediately after breakfast. This time none of us wanted to play. We just sat together on Grandma's bench.

"Will the Red Guards come?" Ji-yun asked.

"Maybe they will, sweetie," Grandma answered. "We just don't know."

She took out her knitting. I tried to to do the same, but I kept finding myself staring into space with no idea of where I was in the pattern. Ji-yun and Ji-yong ran off to play but always came back to the bench after a few minutes. At four o'clock Grandma sent me to see if anything was happening at home.

I cautiously walked into the alley, alert for anything unusual, but there was no sound of drums or gongs or noise at all. The mop was still on the balcony. I looked into our lane. There were no trucks. Everything seemed calm, and I told Grandma it was safe to go home.

Mom and Dad both came home earlier than usual. Dinner was short and nearly silent. Soon after dinner we turned the lights off and got into bed, hoping that the day would end peacefully after all. I lay for a long while without sleeping but finally drifted into a restless doze. When I heard pounding on the door downstairs, I was not sure whether it was real or a dream.

It was real.

I heard my cousin You-mei ask bravely, "Who's there?"

Six-Fingers's voice replied, "The Red Guards. They're here to search your house. Open up!"

They rushed into Fourth Aunt's apartment downstairs.

At first we could not hear much. Then we heard more: doors slamming, a cry from Hua-hua, crash after crash of dishes breaking overhead, and the indistinct voices of the Red Guards.

By this time we were all awake, but no one turned on a light or said anything. We all lay and held our breaths and listened, trying to determine what was going on downstairs. No one even dared to turn over. My whole body was tense. Every sound from my Fourth Aunt's room made me stiffen with dread.

Thirty minutes passed, then an hour. In spite of the fear I began to feel sleepy again.

I was jolted awake by shouts and thunderous knocks. Someone was shouting Dad's name. "Jiang

Xi-reng! Get up! Jiang Xi-reng!"

Dad went to the door. "What do you want?"

"Open up!" Six-Fingers shouted. "This is a search in passing! The Red Guards are going to search your home in passing."

We often asked somebody to buy something in passing or get information in passing, but I had never heard of searching a house in passing.

Dad opened the door.

The first one in was Six-Fingers, wearing an undershirt and dirty blue shorts and flip-flops. Behind him were about a dozen teenaged Red Guards. Though the weather was still quite warm, they all wore tightly belted army uniforms. Their leader was a zealous, loud-voiced girl with short hair and large eyes.

"What's your relationship with the Jiangs living downstairs?" the girl yelled, her hand aggressively on her hip.

"He is her brother-in-law," Six-Fingers answered before Dad could open his mouth.

"Oh, so you're a close relative," she said, as if she only now realized that. "Leniency for confession, severity for resistance! Hand over your weapons now, or we will be forced to search the house." She stood up straight and stared at Dad.

"What weapons?" Dad asked calmly. "We have no—"

"Search!" She cut Dad off with a shouted order and shoved him aside. At the wave of her arm the Red Guards behind her stormed in. Without speaking to each other, they split into three groups and charged toward our drawers, cabinets, and chests. The floor was instantly strewn with their contents.

They demanded that Mom and Dad open anything that was locked, while we children sat on our beds, staring in paralyzed fascination. To my surprise, it was not as frightening as I had imagined through the weeks of waiting. Only Little White was panicked by the crowd and the noise. She scurried among the open chests until she was kicked by a Red Guard. Then she ran up into the attic and did not come down.

I watched one boy going through the wardrobe. He took each piece of clothing off its hanger and threw it onto the floor behind him. He went carefully through a drawer and unrolled the neatly paired socks, tossing them over his shoulder one by one.

I turned my head and saw another boy opening my desk drawer. He swept his hand through it and jumbled everything together before removing the drawer and turning it upside down on the floor. Before he could examine the contents, another one called him away to help move a chest.

All my treasures were scattered on the floor. The butterfly fell out of its glass box; one wing was crushed under a bottle of glass beads. My collection of candy wrappers had fallen out of their notebook and were crumpled under my stamp album.

My stamp album! It had been a birthday gift from Grandma when I started school, and it was my dearest treasure. For six years I had been getting canceled stamps from my friends, carefully soaking them to get every bit of envelope paper off. I had collected them one by one until I had complete sets. I had even bought some inexpensive sets with my own allowance. I loved my collection, even though I knew I should not. With the start of the Cultural Revolution all the stamp shops were closed down, because stamp collecting was considered bourgeois. Now I just knew something terrible was going to happen to it.

I looked at the Red Guards. They were still busy moving the chest. I slipped off the bed and tiptoed across the room. If I could hide it before they saw me . . . I stooped down and reached for the book.

"Hey, what are you doing?" a voice demanded. I

spun around in alarm. It was the Red Guard leader.

"I . . . I didn't do anything," I said guiltily, my eyes straying toward the stamp album.

"A stamp album." She picked it up. "Is this yours?" I nodded fearfully.

"You've got a lot of fourolds for a kid," she sneered as she flipped through it. "Foreign stamps too," she remarked. "You little xenophile."

"I . . . I'm not . . ." I blushed as I fumbled for words.

The girl looked at Ji-yong and Ji-yun, who were still sitting on their beds, watching, and she turned to another Red Guard. "Get the kids into the bathroom so they don't get in the way of the revolution." She threw the stamp album casually into the bag of things to be confiscated and went back downstairs. She didn't even look at me.

Inside the bathroom we could still hear the banging of furniture and the shouting of the Red Guards. Ji-yun lay with her head in my lap, quietly sobbing, and Ji-yong sat in silence.

After a long time the noise died down. Dad opened the bathroom door, and we fearfully came out.

The apartment was a mess. The middle of the floor was strewn with the contents of the overturned chests and drawers. Half of the clothes had been taken away.

The rest were scattered on the floor along with some old copper coins. The chests themselves had been thrown on top of each other when the Red Guards decided to check the walls for holes where weapons could be hidden. Grandma's German clock lay upside down on the floor with the little door on its back torn off.

I looked for my things. The wing of the butterfly had been completely knocked off the body. The bottle holding the glass beads had smashed, and beads were rolling all over the floor. The trampled candy wrappers looked like trash.

And the stamp album was gone forever.

As bad as our apartment was, my Fourth Aunt's apartment was even worse. She had been given lots of fine china when she had married, all of it beautiful and some of it antique. Now it was all destroyed. The Red Guards had carried it up to the roof and smashed it in the big concrete laundry sink. Broken pieces filled the sink and were scattered all over the roof.

Two days after the search we were still cleaning up.

After I put my desk drawer back in order, I began on the wardrobe. One by one I picked up all the clothes, folded them, and put them away. I picked up one of Dad's white shirts and suddenly flushed with embarrassment and anger. My sanitary belt! It was lying on the floor, not even covered by its blue plastic bag. Without thinking, I rolled it up and threw it angrily into the back of the wardrobe.

This, of all things, was private. It was a girl's secret. I never even let Dad or Ji-yong see it. Every time I washed it, I covered it with a towel while it dried in the sun. Now one of those Red Guards, probably a boy, had looked at it—had held it! I felt as if I had been stripped naked in public.

Home, I thought. Wasn't a home a private place? A place where the family could feel secure? How could strangers come and search through our secrets? If Grandpa was a landlord, they could confiscate all his things. But I was not a landlord. Why did they have to search through all *my* things?

I sat on the stool resentfully.

An Yi came in, leaned against a chest, and looked around the ransacked room.

I turned away. I could not bear pity and sympathetic looks, even from An Yi.

She stood for a while and then started to pick up books and put them back on the shelves. She looked thin and fragile. Her face was expressionless.

I suddenly remembered her grandmother under the

white sheet, and everything became clear.

We had a bad class status. That was why An Yi was not allowed to wear mourning bands or even cry aloud for her grandmother. That was why my house was searched, and strangers could come in and do whatever they wanted. It was just a simple fact. Why should I ask why? There was absolutely nothing I could do to change it.

I wiped away my tears and joined An Yi in tidying up the things on the floor.

FATE

A new campaign, "Return to class to promote the revolution," finally took Ji-yong and Ji-yun back to school. Although classes had not gone back to normal, my brother and sister were in school, and that was something.

I was not so lucky. It was almost November, but the junior high school teachers were still out of the city establishing revolutionary ties, and no one could enroll us new students.

I was bored. After finishing the marketing, I read, practiced calligraphy, knitted, and spent a lot of time with An Yi. I was bored, but I never stopped being frightened. I worried about Dad, I worried about Grandma. I worried about An Yi's mother, too. Teacher Wei's situation was very bad. She was a junior high school math teacher, and before the Cultural Revolution she had been a Model Teacher. Her study wall was covered with certificates of merit. Now she was called a black model, and because her father was a capitalist and her mother had committed suicide, she was criticized all the more. The Red Guards at her school held struggle meetings to criticize her almost every day. During those struggle meetings they beat her and whipped her with their belts.

I had seen her coming home, surrounded by an escort of six or seven shouting Red Guards. Her head was bowed down by a sign that read, REACTIONARY MONSTER WEI DONG-LI. She beat a gong and shouted, "I am a reactionary teacher. I am a reactionary monster." While I watched, she stopped shouting and tried to catch her breath. Immediately one of the Red Guards kicked her. Another cuffed her, and she began to croak out her chant once more.

No matter what I did and where I went, the Cultural Revolution followed me.

One cold, windy afternoon I saw Aunt Xi-wen sweeping the street.

She seemed ten years older than the last time I had seen her. Her cheeks were hollow, and she had big bags beneath her eyes. Her once long and curled hair had been cut short and straight, like a country woman's. Outside her padded coat she wore an old blue blouse, loose and faded, with a big patch on the elbow.

She kept her eyes on her work and moved the big broom back and forth laboriously. A gust of wind threatened to scatter the pile of trash she had collected, and she scurried to cover it with her broom to keep it from being blown away. Somehow she tripped over the broom and fell.

It looked like a serious fall. She moved her hand and struggled to get up, but she couldn't seem to stand. I was about to go to help her when I saw her youngest son, my cousin Shan-shan, walking toward us. Shan-shan would help her, and I didn't want to embarrass her by making her realize that I had seen her sweeping the alley. I drew back and walked around them quietly.

After a few steps I turned around to see if they were all right. I could hardly believe my eyes. Shan-shan had walked right past his mother! She was lying there, injured, and he had not stopped to help her. He couldn't possibly have missed her. He must not have wanted to expose himself to criticism by helping someone from a black category.

What a son! I took a step toward Aunt Xi-wen and stopped. Maybe I shouldn't help her either. People would probably say something if they saw me, especially since I was from a black family too. . . .

Before I could decide, Old Mrs. Wang passed by and saw Aunt Xi-wen on the ground. Mrs. Wang hurried over and helped Aunt Xi-wen up. Then Mrs. Wang picked up the broom and dustpan and helped Aunt Xi-wen walk home.

Now I remembered that Shan-shan had written a *da-zi-bao* after their house had been searched, formally breaking relations with his mother. I had admired him for his courage and firmness then.

It was not easy to break with your mother. I could not imagine actually doing it. They had to live in the same room. Would he eat the food she had cooked? Would he speak to her at all?

And what could it be like for Aunt Xi-wen?

One December afternoon when An Yi and I came home from a walk, we saw a big crowd gathered in the middle of our alley. An Yi turned pale and ran to the crowd, dragging me with her.

People, mostly neighbors from the alley, were standing in neat circles, almost as if they had formed ranks intentionally. An oddly familiar voice was shouting, "Down with the oppressor Sang Hong-zhen! Down with the black executioner!" Sang Hong-zhen? Du Hai's mother? The Neighborhood Party Committee Secretary? I looked at An Yi in amazement.

An Yi's whole body relaxed, and she even smiled. "Oh, I was so scared! I thought they were from my mother's school." We squirmed into the crowd.

Du Hai's mother was standing on a stool, her head lowered to her chest. Two torn shoes, the symbol of immorality, were hung around her neck, along with a sign that read, SANG HONG-ZHEN, OPPRESSOR OF THE YOUNG, DESERVES TEN THOUSAND DEATHS. Her disheveled hair dangled around her shocked, gray face. I hardly recognized the once-powerful Neighborhood Party Committee Secretary.

A short man was standing in front of her, shouting so angrily that saliva foamed over his lips. "This damned executioner conned me into going to Xinjiang!" He turned his face toward us. It was a coarse face, and I recognized it at once. He was Xu A-san, who used to live next to Six-Fingers and moved far away to Xinjiang a few years ago. No wonder the voice was familiar.

"She lied to me! She told me Xinjiang was like a flower garden. She said we would live comfortably and eat well. And then what did we find when we got there? Nothing! Not a damned thing! Not even a building to live in. Not even lumber or bricks. We had to build a lousy hut out of dirt. I fell off the roof when we were building it, and now I'm a cripple."

Xu A-san slapped his leg heavily and continued. "When I wrote to her to ask if she could help me come back, she sent my letter to my boss in Xinjiang. They stopped my salary for six months and forced me to write a self-criticism to admit that I was wrong.

"She fooled us into going to Xinjiang and then didn't care whether we lived or died. Is that any way to treat a sixteen-year-old boy? While I was sick and begging for my food in Xinjiang, what was she doing here? She was running around with men and having a good time." The blue veins on his neck stood out, and his pointing finger almost touched her nose. "Thank heaven for the Cultural Revolution. Now I've come back to expose this damned woman and bring the revolution here to our own neighborhood!"

Many of the crowd were moved to tears by Xu A-san's story. I had never liked him or trusted him, but if what he said was true, she was really wicked. Besides, she was Du Hai's mother. What did I care about her problems? Xu A-san was still shouting slogans, but An Yi and I pushed our way out of the struggle meeting.

"I wish I could see Du Hai's face now," I couldn't help gloating.

"Well, you know the old saying. 'The wheel of fate makes a full turn every sixty years,'" An Yi said. "It's their turn to suffer now."

"Does that mean soon it will be our turn to be on top?" I asked thoughtfully.

We walked on in silence. I watched our feet on the pavement. They were perfectly in step.

"Maybe it's really true." It seemed clear to me all of a sudden. "It's just because of fate that we're being hurt. It's just fate that made us be born into black families. And now the wheel of fate is turning. Maybe our families will be free of trouble soon."

When I looked around me, fate seemed to be the only explanation for what was happening.

A few days later Ji-yun was already home from school when I got back from shopping. I tiptoed up behind her and suddenly put my hand in front of her eyes, holding the colored handkerchief I had just bought for her. "Ta-dah!"

To my surprise she did not jump up or cry out with joy.

"Don't you like it? Look at these kittens. Aren't

they cute? It's for you." Collecting colored handkerchiefs was her favorite hobby.

She still did not move.

I went in front of her and was about to tickle her
when I saw her face. She had been crying. Her eyes
were red and swollen, and she had a balled-up handkerchief in her hand.

"What's the matter?"

She did not say a word.

"Why were you crying?"

There was still no answer.

She must be having one of her fits of temper. Ever
since she was little she would cry and refuse to say why.
I knew how to deal with that.

"I'm going to go ask your teacher." I turned around
as if to go.

"No! Don't." She pulled at my clothes.

"Well then, what's wrong?"

"I . . . My . . . schoolbag is gone."

"You lost your schoolbag? What happened?"

She began crying again.

"For goodness' sake, stop crying and tell me what
happened." She kept crying, and I got angry. "You're
really a big girl now, aren't you? You can't even take
care of your schoolbag, and then you just cry about it."

She started wailing, her chest heaving. Grandma rushed in and asked me what was wrong.

"I don't know. She just told me that she lost her schoolbag and then she started crying," I said as I threw the handkerchief angrily onto the table.

"I didn't lose it. . . . It's in the school yard right under the classroom window," Ji-yun said through her sobs.

"What?" Grandma and I asked together. "Why didn't you pick it up?"

"No. I'm not going to pick it up. Some boys in my class threw it out the window. They called me a black whelp. They stood on my desk and said if I stared at them, they would dig my eyes out. They threw it out the window and told me to go pick it up. I won't go."

I did not know what to say. I wished I had not scolded her.

"Why didn't you tell your teacher? She'd make them bring it back," Grandma said.

"That would only make it worse. Last week they were pushing Wei-wei and me around and she told her mother, and she told the teacher, and they were punished. But then they just bullied her even more, and now she has to stay home." Ji-yun's voice was calmer. She had almost stopped crying.

"You should have told Mom and Dad," I said at

last. "They would have done something about this."

"No! They'd just make it worse."

I looked at her with a bad feeling growing inside me. I noticed her lumpy and clumsy braids and felt guilty. She had done them herself. I suddenly felt that I had been too hard on her. I was more like a *da-dui-zhang* than a sister. When I took her to her piano lesson, I scolded her if she did not play well. If she was playing at a friend's house after school, I made her come home and do her homework. In spite of this she trusted me and relied on me for everything. She would ask my advice on what to do or what to wear. If she went to a movie, she wanted me to go with her.

Now she had to learn to take care of herself. It didn't seem fair. She was only ten years old, and too small to protect herself.

I took out the new schoolbag and pencil box I had bought for junior high school. "Here." I put them into her hand. "Let me braid your hair first, and then we'll figure out what else you need and go shopping."

I pondered Ji-yun's fate. She was so little. Why did she have to suffer? And now that the wheel of fate was turning, why hadn't her fate improved?

It had to change soon.

★ ★ ★

A subdued Chinese New Year had passed. So had my thirteenth birthday, which came and went without any celebration. There was a chill to the air that cut into the skin and numbed the body.

I could see Ji-yong and Xiao-cheng standing at the entrance to the alley. They did not seem to feel the cold. Xiao-cheng leaned against a green mailbox, gesturing to Ji-yong. Even at this distance I could feel the confidence in his movements.

Ji-yong had told us that Xiao-cheng's father was having a very difficult time now. Almost every day he was criticized in struggle meetings. In addition, as the highest official of our district before the Cultural Revolution, he was often taken as a companion target to struggle meetings against his junior officers. It could not have been easy for Xiao-cheng to appear so calm.

As I approached them, a row of big trucks came slowly down the street and stopped in front of us.

We were all shocked. Xiao-cheng's father was standing in the first truck.

He was wearing a tall dunce cap covered with red X's, the sign for a criminal. His wrists were tied together behind his back, and his arms were lifted high behind him. His head had been forced down so that we could not see his face. Around his neck was a heavy wooden sign: CAPITALIST EXECUTIONER SHAN YI-DAN. The name had been written in black ink and crossed out in red paint.

We stood there, speechless. The people on the truck shouted slogans, and the trucks moved on. I didn't dare to turn my head and look at Xiao-cheng. I knew that he was very close to his father. I searched for something to say to comfort him, but he spoke first.

"Well, I guess the old man came out to greet his public again."

I stared at him in astonishment. Xiao-cheng's eyes were still following the departing trucks. His lips were set in a mocking smile. I turned and went home without a word.

Was he really used to seeing his father treated like this? Surely he was just hiding his real feelings? I leaned against the balcony railing, trying to clear my head in the chilly air. I didn't notice Ji-yong until he leaned on the railing next to me. His face looked very strained.

"Ming-ming's father is dead," he said weakly.

"What?" I shivered.

"The Institute called his mother early this morning. They said that he hanged himself."

"Hanged himself?"

Ji-yong nodded. "The Institute didn't even let her see

the body except through a window. Then they had the body cremated. Xiao-cheng was saying that they probably beat him to death before he 'hanged himself.'. . . There's Ming-ming. I've got to go."

Ming-ming and Xiao-cheng were waiting down in the alley. When Ji-yong got there, the three of them walked off together.

I went inside, but I still felt very cold.

An Yi opened the door. Before I could mention Ming-ming's father, I noticed her eyes. They were red and swollen.

"What happened?"

She went back inside their apartment without answering, leaving the door open for me.

I had not been inside their apartment for a long time. Since Grandma had died, her ninety-year-old sister sat blankly in front of the window all day and never left the room. The mahogany furniture that had filled the place was gone, confiscated. The room seemed larger, and our steps echoed. An Yi and I sat by the window on the old stools that were now their only seats.

"What's wrong?" I asked again.

"My mom . . ." She dropped her eyes.

"Beaten again?"

"Worse than that. Yesterday the teachers who were under investigation had to climb the factory chimney." She choked and could not continue.

"Climb the chimney?" I was aghast. "What kind of remolding is that? Did she . . . did she do it?"

"She didn't dare not to. That would be resisting the revolution—she would have been beaten to . . ." An Yi choked again. "Luckily the factory was off yesterday. You know how hot . . . the chimney gets. . . . She couldn't have . . ."

I couldn't say a word.

"I'm really afraid, Ji-li." An Yi looked straight into my eyes. "If Mom is a little late coming back from school, we're so worried. Dad paces up and down, and I just can't do anything. Sometimes Dad can't stand it anymore, and he goes to school to meet her. I'm so scared. I don't know what'll happen next. Ji-li, sometimes I'm really afraid to go home." The expression in her eyes made me want to cry.

I saw her mother clinging to the high chimney. I shivered. I saw her grandma standing by the window in her black clothes; Old Qian, collapsed at the foot of the propaganda wall; Xiao-cheng's father, arms wrenched behind his back; Ming-ming's father, dangling in the air, his tongue dangling out of his bruised, purple face.

Fate.

An Yi dried her tears. We sat in silence for a long time before I asked, "Did . . . do you ever blame your mother for all this?"

"I don't know. Sometimes I think she's just too pushy, like when she dismissed her students' Lei Feng Study Group. That's what first made them call her a reactionary. It made trouble for all of us. But she really did do it for her students' own good. That Lei Feng Study Group was a joke. They didn't study his good deeds. They just fooled around every day, and their grades got worse and worse. She wasn't reactionary at all."

"I hate my grandfather!" I said suddenly. "If he hadn't been a landlord, none of this would have happened to me. . . . But I guess the only thing I can do is stop thinking about it. It's just my fate that I was born in these times."

"That's it," An Yi agreed. "But why doesn't our fate change?"

I had an idea. "Listen, let's predict the future. My cousin told me how to do it. We write different things on different pieces of paper and put them on the windowsill. The first one to blow off will come true."

Predicting the future was fourolds, but we could not help doing it anyway. We prepared three pieces of paper: EVERYTHING WILL GET BETTER, BAD LUCK WILL CONTINUE, and SOME GOOD AND SOME BAD THINGS WILL HAPPEN. We folded them, put a little water on each one, and then stuck them on the sill.

We waited for the wind to blow from heaven while I prayed silently, "May Allah bless us. May Allah bless us. May Allah bless us." A breeze rustled the folded papers, but none blew off. Another breeze came. One of the papers blew off the sill. An Yi caught it before it hit the floor.

"Which one?" I asked. "Which one?"

She unfolded the paper. "Some good and some bad."

We looked at each other, and neither of us said anything.

JUNIOR HIGH SCHOOL AT LAST

After more than a year the great day had finally arrived: my first day of junior high school!

It was a warm September morning. Four hundred brand-new students made the auditorium of Xin-zha Junior High School even stuffier. Some of us had not seen each other for more than a year, and everyone was excitedly picking old classmates out of the sea of new faces. The new school chairman, who had replaced the old principal, was giving us a welcome speech, but we had too much to catch up with among ourselves to pay him much attention.

An Yi and I leaned forward to hear the boy with protruding ears in the row in front of us. ". . . In my brother's factory the fighting was really serious. Two factions were fighting to lead the revolution in the factory. They both got guns from the army. People were killed with machine guns. My brother saw it with his own eyes. . . ." Someone pulled my braid, and I turned around. Deng Yi-yi, no longer dressed like a pauper, was smiling at us.

"What a beautiful sweater," I said. "Did you make it yourself?"

"My older sister made it for me. It's a new pattern called 'double pearls.'" She proudly stretched her arm out to give us a closer look.

An Yi grabbed her arm and patted it three times. "New clothes, new clothes, one, two, three," she chanted, just as we had when we were little. We all giggled.

"Are you two inseparables in the same class?" Deng Yi-yi teased.

"No," I said sadly. "I'm in class four and she's in class six. What about you?"

"I'm in class nine."

"Do you happen to know what class Yang Fan is in?" An Yi glanced nervously at Yang Fan, sitting off to our right.

"I think she's in class two."

"What about Du Hai?" I asked, trying to control my anxiety.

"I don't know about the boys."

"What about Yin Lan-lan, then?" I asked. "You know about her, don't you?"

"She's in my class," Chen Yi-yi said.

My eyes met An Yi's. Ever since we had received our admission letters, we had worried about being in the same class as those three. Now we did not have to worry about two of them. If only Du Hai could be kept far away from us too. . . .

The chairman finished his speech.

We all crowded out of the auditorium and rushed, laughing and shouting, toward the new classroom building.

"Let's go home together after class," An Yi called as we separated at the third floor. "Meet me downstairs."

I stopped at room 301. This was my classroom. I paused nervously, wondering about my new classmates and my teachers. Would fate be kind to me? I peeked into the doorway. There were already quite a few people sitting at their places. I looked at the seating chart on the blackboard and went straight to my desk. My deskmate, a plump girl with long pigtails, smiled at me and nodded.

My heart was pounding. I looked around the class. There was no one I knew. I scanned the seating chart again. None of my former classmates were in this class. No one in this class knew about my class status! I could make a new start and just be a person like everyone else.

I wanted to laugh out loud. Instead I smiled broadly at my new deskmate.

The classroom was much more spacious than my classroom in Xin Er Primary School, and brighter. Facing the street were three big windows, and I could see the trees and housetops across the way. The desks and chairs were made of iron and painted orange. The huge blackboard was made of real slate. It gave off a sharp sound when you tapped it, and it would not need to be painted regularly like the wooden ones we had in primary school.

As I was still surveying the room, a slim man walked in. The class immediately quieted down.

"I'm your homeroom teacher. My name is Zhang Xin." As soon as he started speaking, the students murmured to each other. We were all delighted. His voice was so gentle and his face was so young. He was sure to be an easygoing teacher. He picked up a piece of chalk and wrote two characters, "Zhang Xin," in the corner of the blackboard. The rustling stopped at once, and the room became dead quiet. His writing was beautiful and powerful, and the lively and vigorous flourishes in his calligraphy awed us. His handwriting and his voice revealed two completely different personalities.

Besides introducing himself, Teacher Zhang spoke

only three sentences: Welcome to class four; he would teach us English; and we would spend the whole first two weeks in Political Study, reading Central Committee documents and Chairman Mao's works. The day ended with that. It was far less exciting than I had imagined. What a strange teacher, I thought. Full of contradictions and stingy with words. I had thought that he would at least give us a tour of the school.

I waited for quite a while before An Yi's class was over. She was overjoyed because Du Hai was not in her class either.

It was a beautiful fall day. Even the two plain buildings looked particularly pleasant. The parasol trees lining the sidewalks were straight and tall and seemed to smile at us in the bright sunshine.

For more than a year I had waited at home, bored and depressed by all the news of fighting, and by the struggles at Mom's and Dad's work units. Now all that was over. Finally I was in junior high school. Though it was not as large as Shi-yi, not as elegant as Shi-yi, I was excited beyond words.

The lovely November sunshine crept into the classroom, shining warmly upon the beautifully written but boring English words on the blackboard.

DOWN WITH IMPERIALISM!

DOWN WITH REVISIONISM!

DOWN WITH THE NEW TSARS!

Teacher Zhang moved his homemade bamboo pointer slowly along these sentences. Over and over, we repeated after him. Some read quickly, some slowly, some at a high pitch, and some low. It was a thoroughly unpleasant chorus. When we read, "Down with the new tsars!" someone deliberately dragged out the English phrase and turned it into Chinese, *niu-zha-zi*, beef crackling. The whole class burst out in laughter, and others gleefully imitated him.

I glanced at my deskmate, Chang Hong. She was busily writing a speech. I rested my chin upon my hand and sighed.

This was the sixth English class of the term. In the first class Teacher Zhang had told us that in order to integrate all aspects of our study with the revolution and to prepare for war, we would learn military and political terms first. When he started with "Lay down your arms and we will spare your lives," we were quite interested. Now, after six periods, we had learned "Long live Chairman Mao," "Long live the Chinese Communist Party," and "Long live socialist China." We had learned "Stand up," "Sit down," and "Hands up."

Today we were learning "Down with." It was boring, and we knew that if we did not learn grammar instead of just phrases, we would never learn English.

I watched two sparrows twittering and hopping merrily among the naked branches outside the classroom window.

When I was little, I had dreamed about attending junior high school. I had heard about the spacious classrooms, the tall buildings, and the huge, well-equipped gymnasiums. It was fascinating to think about all the things you could learn there: Galileo's acceleration experiment, the dissection of rabbits, and making materials change state in a test tube. Junior high schools seemed to be wonderful and mysterious palaces.

Now that I had entered the palace, I was disappointed. All the classes except for mathematics were completely uninteresting. We had no textbooks, only hastily compiled mimeographed handouts. English class was a bore. Politics class was actually just the familiar Communist Party history. Physics, Chemistry, and Biology had been replaced by Fundamentals of Industry and Agriculture, because of Chairman Mao's instruction to "combine education with practical experience." One day the teacher had brought the wrong handouts to class. He had prepared a lesson on raising pigs, but he had mistakenly brought the handouts

titled "The Close-Planting System of Rice Growing."
He stood awkwardly on the platform for a minute or
two, then dismissed the class. The poor teachers!
Trained in the traditional sciences, they were totally lost
when trying to teach us about pigs *or* paddy fields.

I heard a roar of laughter from the back of the class.
Probably someone had told another joke. I raised my
head and saw Teacher Zhang standing with his back
toward us, reading all by himself, "Down with imperialism." A boy sitting in the last row threw something
to another boy halfway across the room. Pudge was
hunched over crocheting a tablecloth under her desk.
Four-Eyes had taken his glasses off, rested his head on
his desk, and begun to snore loudly.

The bell rang. I put my pencil box into my desk and
stood up to stretch.

"Attention, please." Teacher Zhang rapped his
pointer on his desk. "Next period will be a study hall.
You can study Chairman Mao's works by yourselves."
He had to speak loudly to be heard. He was probably
as tired of reading newspapers and Central Committee
documents as we were, so he had decided to let us while
away the time by ourselves. It was disgraceful.

A boy in the front row turned around and made a
face at the rest of the class.

Suddenly a voice asked, "Teacher Zhang, since it's self-study, can we go home to do it?" The whole class fell silent. We looked around and saw Bai Shan's tall, thin form standing beside his desk. He looked straight at Teacher Zhang, with his face as frank and sincere as usual.

Teacher Zhang stared back at Bai Shan. At first he looked a little uncomfortable, but after a few seconds of silence he said calmly, "You can go home if you're sure you'll study."

Bai Shan unhurriedly put his things in his schoolbag and said, "I'm sure." He left the classroom with his unfashionable blue rayon jacket fluttering as he walked.

The class exploded in chatter.

"What kind of attitude is that? It's insulting to Chairman Mao." Chang Hong was quite indignant.

"He said he would study at home." I disagreed with her. I understood his anger about the English class. In fact, I admired him, and I was glad that he had the courage to do something about it.

I remembered our last Physical Education class. As a part of our preparation for war we were supposed to practice crawling under wires and climbing over wooden obstacles. When the teacher had asked the boys to get the gym mats, the boys had just looked at each other without moving. Without respect, what could the poor man do? At this embarrassing moment, Bai Shan had caught the eye of his two best friends. The three of them had moved toward the mats, and all at once the rest of the boys followed them.

I found him a very interesting boy.

A cold December drizzle was falling as I stood in my place and listened to the loud blare of the prelude music for our daily exercises. I rolled up my collar and stuffed my hands into my pockets, but I could not stop shivering. It seemed that winter had come overnight.

Though my eyes were fixed on the back of the head lined up in front of me, Grandma's worried voice still echoed in my mind. "Your dad has been sent to political study class."

For the last week or two, Dad had been coming home very late every night. Sometimes even before he ate, he and Mom would go into the bathroom and shut the door while they talked. We heard their muffled voices discuss bad news: Uncle Zhu had been detained by the theater while they investigated his suspected counterrevolutionary activities. Aunt Wu had been detained too, even though her only crime was having had relations with other men before she married Uncle Tian.

Dad smoked in the bathroom as he paced up and down. Whenever Mom opened the door, the heavy odor of tobacco rolled out. Other times he would sit at the desk without a smile, writing silently while cigarette smoke filled the apartment.

I knew that Dad's political study class, like mine, studied Chairman Mao's works and Party Central Committee documents. But unlike mine, the purpose of his class was to make the participants confess their mistakes or crimes. Only people whose mistakes were very serious were sent to these classes.

What mistakes had Dad made, other than having a landlord for a father? Could he really be a rightist after all? I clenched my fists in my pockets. The family problems seemed to grow on my back like a tumor, and whatever I did, they just grew worse.

The music stopped. "Now let's begin our Morning Benediction. Please get your Precious Red Books ready." A familiar voice interrupted my thoughts.

My deskmate, Chang Hong, was standing on the platform. It was her turn to lead the morning exercises again. She was wearing her favorite green army uniform, and the belt around her waist made her look even plumper than usual. Even from the last row I could see her glowing red cheeks. She was a celebrity now, newly elected to the Red Guards Committee, one of only nine people elected by all the Red Guards in the school. Ever since she had joined the Committee, I had felt myself pulling away from her, even though I admired her more. She was nice enough—frank, sincere, and sympathetic. But as a child from a black family—a black whelp—I felt awkward around a Red Guard leader.

"Now let's sincerely and wholeheartedly wish long life to our great leader, great teacher, great commander, and great helmsman, Chairman Mao." Her emotional voice blared from the loudspeaker, and I reached into my pocket for my Precious Red Book.

It was not there.

I had forgotten to put it back in my pocket after I had washed my jacket yesterday. And standing right behind me was the head of the school, Chairman Jin, who had repeatedly stressed the importance of the Morning Benediction. If he found out that I had forgotten to bring my Precious Red Book, would he give me trouble? Would he criticize me in front of the entire school? I froze. I couldn't decide whether to wave my hand without the Precious Red Book or to put my hand down.

Something red flashed in front of me and the plastic cover of a Precious Red Book was in my hand. In relief

I clutched the cover, which looked just like the red book from a distance, and waved my hand three times. "Long life to Chairman Mao! Long life! Long life!" I shouted with my classmates.

I looked gratefully at my rescuer. To my surprise it was my classmate Sun Lin-lin. Her thick glasses reflected the light as she looked to the front. She repeated the chant, waving her coverless Precious Red Book as if nothing had happened.

I never would have guessed that Lin-lin—so quiet in class that I hardly knew she was there—would be so sharp. If I had been in her position, I thought, I would never even have noticed the problem, let alone come up with such a quick solution.

As soon as exercises were over, I turned to Lin-lin and put the cover in her hand. "Thanks a lot! You really saved my life!"

She made no answer, just shook her head slightly and smiled shyly.

"Chairman Jin was right behind me. I was scared out of my wits."

She still said nothing, but she did smile a little more broadly. With her short, naturally curly hair and her light-yellow corduroy jacket, she looked like a little doll, a lovely doll with glasses.

The classroom was quiet. Everyone was paying close attention to Teacher Li's low voice. It was always a relief when Math class started. Teacher Li was over fifty years old, and her hoarse voice was not very loud, but when she stood before the class, she seemed so intent and serious that we had to listen to her. We were impressed by the fact that she had been teaching for almost thirty years and had been a Model Teacher year after year, and by the rumor that she had never married, and had devoted her whole life to her teaching. The fact that she insisted on using her own lecture notes with added quotations from Chairman Mao instead of the mimeographed handouts made us respect her even more.

"Generally speaking, the results of this test were better than the last." Teacher Li cleared her throat and unconsciously brushed her right sleeve with her left hand. After years of doing that every time she used the blackboard, she did it now even when there was no chalk dust there to brush off. "Five students failed, and two, Bai Shan and Jiang Ji-li, got one hundred percent."

"Wow, a hundred again. That's great!" Chang Hong cried out, and slapped me heartily on the back.

Teacher Li stopped talking. The whole class turned

to look at me. I wanted to give Chang Hong a big kick.

Then I saw the expression in their eyes. Every face was friendly. Chang Hong expressed her admiration openly and directly. Lin-lin's shy smile was genuinely glad, and Bai Shan's look was one of sincere congratulation. Even Teacher Li's usually serious face was smiling slightly.

It felt almost like a dream from long ago. I remembered another Ji-li, one who was always praised by her teachers and respected by her classmates. A Ji-li who always pushed herself to do better, achieve more.

For once I forgot my worries and smiled with my whole heart.

Time always passed too quickly in math class. Teacher Li was closing her notebook when she remembered a note that was in it.

"Oh, there's a message. Jiang Ji-li and Bai Shan, please stay after class. Teacher Zhang would like to speak with you." She put the note back in her book and turned to clean the blackboard.

Suddenly I felt nervous again. Had I done something wrong? Did this have something to do with my class status?

My classmates were also uneasy. They all turned their eyes toward Teacher Li. The whole room felt tense.

Teacher Li finished erasing the blackboard and turned around, brushing her right sleeve with her left hand. "What's wrong?" she asked in surprise.

No one said anything. Chang Hong glanced anxiously at me and twisted her pencil.

"Oh, are you worried about Teacher Zhang seeing Jiang Ji-li and Bai Shan? It's nothing bad. He just wants to talk to them about joining the propaganda group for the blackboard newspaper, because they both have beautiful handwriting."

The class burst out laughing. I laughed with them, at Teacher Li who had not made the message clear, at my own fears, at the whole false alarm.

I saw several classmates turning to look at me. Bai Shan's deskmate whispered in his ear and got a joking punch in return.

Then I stopped laughing.

I remembered primary school, the praises and the honors. But what had I gotten in the end? People were jealous because I was favored. I remembered the humiliating talk with the Red Successors, the terrible accusations of the *da-zi-bao*. Why should I go through that again? High grades, propaganda group—and then what? When they found out about my family background, they would treat me just as Du Hai and Yin

Lan-lan had. And Bai Shan and I were conspicuous enough in class. If we did the blackboard newspaper together, people would start to gossip about us.

Class was over. I grabbed Chang Hong's arm as she was leaving.

"Will you do me a favor? Tell Teacher Zhang that I couldn't wait to see him."

"Why not?" She looked surprised.

"I have to go home and make dinner, and I have a lot of housework to do every day. I don't have time to do the blackboard newspaper." Without waiting for her response, I picked up my schoolbag and headed for the door.

LOCKED UP

Winter vacation had started, and we children all stayed at home.

At eleven o'clock one night Mom and Dad were still in the bathroom, where they had been talking ever since Dad had come home from work. Ji-yong and Ji-yun were asleep, and Grandma was in bed reading the newspaper. I was trying to finish *Jane Eyre*.

Someone knocked softly on the door. I listened, and it came again: two soft taps, followed by a whispered, "Lao Jiang! Lao Jiang!" Only Dad's friends from the theater called him that.

"Who is it?" I walked to the door and called quietly.

"It's me, Fan Wen-chong."

I opened the door, happy to see him. "Uncle Fan, it's so late— Oh my!" I stopped when I saw his face. It was swollen, bruised, and bloody. Standing in the dark doorway, he looked like a monster. He swayed back and forth weakly, and as I stared, his face crumpled into tears. I turned away and ran to my bed.

The whole family was startled by my cry. Grandma was trembling as she got out of bed and pulled him into the bathroom to wash his bruises. Ji-yong and Ji-yun huddled together at the bathroom door, while Mom and Dad went downstairs to bring his bicycle into the building before the neighbors could see it.

I huddled on a corner of the bed, not wanting to look at him again, not wanting to see his humiliation. I thought of his expressive face, handsome and vigorous. I remembered his huge success in many shows, the flowers and admirers. His students and other actors used to defer to him so respectfully. Where were his dignity and authority now? Where was Uncle Fan?

I curled up as if I were the one being showered with blows.

"Come on, get back into bed. Children shouldn't be so nosy." Grandma dragged Ji-yong and Ji-yun back into the room.

"Grandma, how's Uncle Fan?" I whispered.

"He's all right." She looked very tired. "You go to sleep now. Don't mention this to anyone, anyone at all. Understand?" Grandma tucked our quilts around us, then turned out the light and went back to the bathroom.

The frequent tossing and turning told me that no one had gone back to sleep.

"Ji-li, Uncle Fan groaned when Grandma washed his face." Ji-yun broke the silence.

"His hands were shaking," Ji-yong said after a while.

"Grandma told you to go to sleep and not be so nosy. Why don't you just shut up?" I did not know why I was suddenly so angry.

Lying in the darkness, I could hear the faint voices in the bathroom. I tried to close my eyes, but when I did, all I could see was Uncle Fan's deformed face. Suddenly the voices in the bathroom grew louder. I held my breath and listened closely.

"That's nonsense! How could you do that?" Dad said.

"You know. They use psychological pressure."

"That doesn't mean that you should make up a story about something you never did!" Dad's voice grew still louder.

"So what if I never listened to foreign radio broadcasts? They'll stop beating me if I confess to it, won't they? 'Leniency to those who confess, and severity to those who resist.' Look at my face, Lao Jiang. I can't stand it anymore. . . ."

The voice trailed off, and I thought I heard sobbing.

I pulled my quilt over my head and tried to block out the sounds. This was not my Uncle Fan. My Uncle Fan would not listen to foreign radio broadcasts or worry about psychological pressure. Most of all, I knew that my Uncle Fan would never cry.

I began crying to myself under the quilt. I did not know why.

Three days after he had come to our house, Uncle Fan had been detained. Since then, every evening, Mom and Grandma had fidgeted, going to the kitchen on the landing, finding something to do on the roof, unable to relax as they waited for Dad to come home.

It was getting darker and darker. Ji-yun sat under the light doing her math homework. I worked on the sweater I was knitting for Dad, sharing the sofa with Ji-yong, who was intent on making a periscope.

My fingers moved mechanically. My mind was far away from what I was doing.

I had just read an article in the paper. It told of a "historical counterrevolutionary," who as a local official before Liberation had killed two Communist guerrillas. The paper explained that because he had confessed and had a positive attitude, he was pardoned. Meanwhile an "active counterrevolutionary" was convicted of slandering the Red Guards. He refused to confess and was imprisoned.

So this was their policy of psychological pressure. No wonder Uncle Fan thought he should confess to something he had not done. Had he confessed to listening to foreign broadcasts? If he had, why hadn't he been treated with leniency? Why had he been detained? I could not figure it out.

Finally we heard steps on the stairs, and we all held our breaths while we watched the door. It opened, and there was Dad. I looked at his face, body, and legs. No bruises. We all sighed with relief.

"I can't take it anymore. Today at the meeting they were obviously referring to me." As soon as he walked in the door, Dad started talking excitedly and nervously to Mom and Grandma, not even caring that we children were listening. "They stressed again and again that they already had enough information and they would give the person one last chance to confess. If he continued to hold back, they would have to name him publicly, and he would lose his chance at leniency."

The adults went into the bathroom together and closed the door, but we could still hear them talking.

"Well, do you want to confess then? It might be better than being punished." Grandma's voice sounded unusually old.

"But I have no idea what they want me to confess."

After a pause Mom's voice said, "How about leaving the Party—"

Dad cut her short. "No. I did nothing wrong. How can I confess?"

I stopped knitting and looked up in alarm. Leaving the Party? What was that? Ji-yong and Ji-yun had tilted their heads to hear better.

"What about Fan Wen-chong coming to our house?" Mom asked. "He might have confessed he visited us. Maybe that's what they meant when they said they already had the information. . . . They could say we were establishing counterrevolutionary ties."

"Of course you won't mention that. That would be betraying a friend." Grandma was firm. "We promised not to tell anyone. Wen-chong has been a friend for over thirty years, and he certainly won't say anything. We won't say anything either."

"But what if the theater decides to punish him?" Mom asked.

There was no answer. I could hear Dad pacing around the room, and I could smell the cigarette smoke coming through the crack under the door.

I started to knit again. It was the same story day after day: restlessness, anxiety, the adults' arguments. It was nearly Chinese New Year, and no one even mentioned it.

I wanted to know what was going on, but I was afraid to hear any more bad news. I suddenly wished I could live at school. Then I could forget what was happening, and I could laugh again. I wished that I had been born into a trouble-free family.

Very early on Chinese New Year's morning Grandma shook me awake. She was in tears.

"Your dad never came home last night. He's been locked up." Grandma laid her head on my pillow and continued to weep.

I stared at Grandma's face, and my fingers tightened on the sleeve of my pajamas. He had not come home for the New Year's Eve dinner, though we had waited until ten o'clock. We had gone to bed hoping that he would come later.

"He knew that he would be detained sooner or later. He told me not to worry too much." Grandma's voice was steady, but her tears kept dropping on my hand. Now I began crying too.

"Why?" Ji-yong was awake too. "What did they lock him up for?"

"I have no idea. I'm sure your father hasn't done anything wrong," Grandma said.

Mom's weak voice was calling me. I jumped out of bed, threw on my padded coat, and ran over to her. Dad's side of the quilt was untouched and the pillow was smooth. Mom lay in bed with her eyes tightly shut, her face a waxy yellow. I knew what that meant. She was having an attack of Ménière's disease. She had had it for years, and an attack could come on at any time. The world would spin around her and she would feel weak and nauseous. Even opening her eyes would make her helplessly dizzy.

"How are you feeling, Mom?" I gently stroked the hand that was outside the quilt. "Would you like some soy milk? I'll tell Ji-yong to go buy some."

"No, no. I want you to give Uncle Tian a call. He might know what happened to your dad." Mom fumbled under her pillow for her address book and handed it to me.

A little before seven I bundled up and dashed out into the cold.

In other years on New Year's morning the streets would be littered with shreds of colored firecracker paper. Soon after breakfast people loaded with gifts would begin to stream out of their homes to wish friends and relatives a happy New Year. This year firecrackers were fourolds, and few people were in the mood to celebrate. Streets were so quiet that the city seemed almost deserted.

Following Mom's instructions, I went to a telephone kiosk a few blocks from our alley so the neighbors would not overhear me asking about Dad. I waited, shivering, for the workers in Uncle Tian's kiosk to fetch him.

"Uncle Tian, it's me, Ji-li," I said eagerly as soon as he got to the phone.

"Oh, Ji—" He stopped abruptly. "How are you?" he asked in his actor's voice. I could tell he was afraid people at his phone kiosk were listening.

"Mom asked me to call to wish you Happy New Year, and to ask about things at work, and about Dad and all." He was so guarded that I wanted to be vague too.

"Yesterday at the meeting they mentioned his name. He's stubborn, you know. He wouldn't talk about radio or establishing ties, so they lost patience. He— I've got to go. 'Bye." He hung up.

Strong gusts of wind blew against me. I lowered my

head and leaned forward to fight my way home.

Grandma was waiting for me on the stairs. Inside, I told Mom and Grandma what Uncle Tian had said. Mom looked even paler.

"Establishing counterrevolutionary ties and listening to foreign radio? It must be Fan Wen-chong who told them," Grandma said slowly. "It must be. The radio was his idea, and he's the only one who's come here." Her voice grew indignant. "Foreign radio! How could we listen to foreign radio? We haven't had a short-wave radio for thirty years, since the Japanese invaded. Fan's lying!"

"Mother, Mother. Calm down." Mom patted Grandma feebly. "We don't want the neighbors to hear. Don't worry too much. When I feel better, I'll go to the theater and ask."

I went out to the kitchen to be alone.

It was freezing cold, and there was no food prepared, not even hot water. The frost patterns on the window were as beautiful as always, but I could not appreciate them. Every other New Year's morning the kitchen would be bustling. Mom and Grandma would be making dumplings and my birthday noodles; we kids would be running in and out in our new clothes. Every guest who came to our home on New Year's Day would also bring me a birthday gift. I always felt the whole country was celebrating my birthday.

Today I was fourteen. I started to write "Happy Birthday" on the frosted windows. The melted ice dripped down the window slowly and crookedly, like tears.

Late that evening I woke up and saw Grandma on her knees, mumbling quietly. "May Allah protect my son," I heard her say. Then she wearily climbed into bed.

I sat on a bench outside the conference room of the district office of Mom's store. Nervously, I fiddled with my coat buttons. On our way here Mom had been so still and quiet that I was frightened too. She had fainted again yesterday. She was really too weak to go out, but still her office had called to insist that she come. And Grandma had insisted that she take me with her.

Mom's office was in a building that had been a big house before Liberation. The narrow hallway was painted white, but the paint showed some stains. I stared at them. I could not hear what they were saying inside, but I knew it would not be anything good since they had received Mom so coldly and treated me so brusquely.

I could not help thinking of Dad. We had not seen him for days. I pictured him stubbornly refusing to confess. What was he supposed to confess? Uncle Fan's visit? Was that a crime? I was frightened. They would probably beat him, I thought. I saw Uncle Fan's battered face. And the terrible image of a still, dangling shape . . . Ming-ming's father. . . .

I heard a man's voice raised above the others, and the words "your husband." They were talking about Dad! Without thinking, I slid down the bench to hear better. "Your refusal to help us is a very bad sign. Your husband's unit would not take such a step without very good evidence, and it is not likely that he could do it without your knowing. Your own position is very tenuous, you know."

A woman's voice was speaking, and I strained to hear. " . . . if you're as stubborn as your husband, we may have to take stronger actions. I'm sure you don't want that any more than we do."

I could not hear Mom's reply. I leaned even closer to the door. Mom's voice was only the faintest murmur.

The man's voice, even louder than before, was like an assault.

"Then there is nothing more to say until you decide to be reasonable. I'm sure your husband's unit will resume paying his salary when he confesses, and we will return yours to its former level when you decide to cooperate. I'm sure we will speak again soon." The door banged open and a cold-faced man strode out. He did not even glance at me. Two women also walked out of the room. One of them looked straight at me and sneered before she turned back to her companion.

Mom did not come out. I peeked in the door. She had collapsed on the table. "Mom! Mom!" I shouted in panic as I ran to her. Her eyes were closed tightly and her forehead was covered with beads of sweat despite the cold weather. "How are you feeling, Mom? Do you want some water?" I wiped her forehead with my handkerchief and stroked her back gently. Finally, without raising her head, she said weakly, "Don't worry, I'm all right."

Mom sat silently on my bike luggage rack, weak and pale. She bent over my seat and rested her arm on my shoulder. I clenched the handlebar tightly and walked the bike very slowly. I heard the distant whistle of a passing train, and I wished I could get on it and go far away, to a place without struggle meetings, without class status, without confessions.

★ ★ ★

We had not seen or heard from Dad in a week since he had been detained. Mom asked me to take some clothes to him.

The Children's Art Theater was on Hua-shan Road, in a neighborhood that hardly seemed part of the city. Before Liberation only the wealthiest had lived here, in grand mansions set back from the street behind sturdy walls. Two rows of trees stretched their branches toward the sky, reaching across the trolley wires and holding hands with their sisters on the other side, giving the street a huge green parasol in the summertime.

I had always liked visiting Dad's theater. I enjoyed walking on the beautiful street, and I loved poking around inside the building, with its fascinating secrets.

But today the trees were bare. Not a soul could be seen on the street, and the theater seemed like a dark cave that waited to swallow anyone who dared approach.

When I left home, I tried to seem relaxed. I did not want Mom and Grandma to worry. But inside I was trembling. I did not want to go. But Grandma had been married to a landlord and Mom was in trouble because of Dad. I did not dare imagine what might happen if they went.

I stopped outside the office to gather my courage

once more. Finally I tiptoed up to the reception desk. It was tall, almost too tall for me to see over. I raised my head and looked timidly at the receptionist.

"What do you want?" he asked without any expression.

"I came to see my father, Jiang Xi-reng." I held up the parcel Grandma had packed.

"Oh, Jiang Xi-reng's daughter." Neither his face nor his voice showed any emotion at all. "You're not allowed to see him. Leave your things here."

I hesitated for a second. Then I struggled to raise my package to the counter.

He emptied it onto the desk and quickly sorted through it: a few clothes, a woolen sweater I had just finished knitting, toothpaste, soap, a towel, and a jar of Grandma's fresh beef chili sauce. He put everything back in the bag except the chili sauce.

"No food is allowed." His cold tone told me no discussion was allowed either.

I took the still-warm jar in my hands and bit my lips. "Please, can I see my dad? Just for a moment? I won't say anything to him, I promise."

"I said no!" he snapped. "That's the rule."

"What's the matter?" Someone came out of the door behind the desk: a short, thin man with closely cropped hair. I did not know his name, but I recognized him as the foreman of the scene shop.

"This is Jiang Xi-reng's daughter. She's pestering me to see her father."

"Jiang Xi-reng . . ." He narrowed his eyes and looked at me with a calculating expression. His face was so thin that the skin seemed stretched over his cheekbones. His eyes were not large, but they were fierce and penetrating.

He frightened me. I stepped back from the desk and turned to go.

"All right. Follow me." His answer stunned me and astonished the receptionist. I followed close behind him into a hallway, hoping that he would not change his mind.

We went up and down and made several turns before we finally reached the dance studio. Three walls of the huge hall were covered by mirrors. The fourth contained a row of French windows looking out onto the spacious theater grounds below. The man pointed out the window.

There was Dad.

Even at a distance and in the poor light I recognized him immediately. He was carrying a large concrete pipe on his shoulder with Uncle Fan and two other men. His back was more stooped than I remembered, and he was awkwardly using his hands to take the weight of the pipe off his shoulder.

I wiped the tears away from my eyes and pressed my forehead against the window, trying to see more clearly.

At least he was still alive. At least he was still able to work. He wasn't lying on the floor, bruised and cut from beatings, as Grandma had imagined. But it was cold, and he was wearing only his old coffee-colored jacket. I hoped they would let him wear the new sweater I had brought him.

"All right, you've seen your father." The thin man's voice was cold. "Now I want to have a talk with you."

He led me into the small conference room next door and motioned for me to sit down across the table from him.

"You saw your father. He is being remolded through labor. We have evidence that he has committed a serious counterrevolutionary crime." He paused and fixed me with his eyes. "But he is very stubborn and refuses to confess. And your mother. Humph. She's another despicable thing!"

"She's not a thing, she's a human being," I wanted to scream, but I knew that I should not provoke him.

He could have me arrested, he could never let me see Dad again, he could beat Dad. . . . I stared at the table.

"You are different from your parents. You were born and raised in New China. You are a child of Chairman Mao. You can choose your own destiny: You can make a clean break with your parents and follow Chairman Mao, and have a bright future; or you can follow your parents, and then . . . you will not come to a good end." As he spoke the last phrase, he paused meaningfully after each word.

I nodded. I could hardly breathe. All I wanted was to get away from there as fast as I could.

"Do you have anything to say?"

I shook my head quickly.

"You think it over. If you think of something, you can always come to talk to us," he said.

AN EDUCABLE CHILD

Grandma cried whenever she thought about Dad, and Mom was not getting any better, so I stayed home to help. While Ji-yong and Ji-yun were in school during the day, I shopped and sewed and worried. It was hard for me to keep my mind off Dad and the scene-shop foreman's threats.

The German clock struck four times. I was finishing the last sleeve of a jacket for Ji-yun before starting to make dinner when I heard a soft voice calling me from the alley. Who could it be? An Yi always came directly upstairs, and none of my junior high school friends knew where I lived. I put down the sleeve and went to the French window.

It was Lin-lin, eye-catching in her yellow corduroy jacket. She was shivering in the freezing wind. After a false spring the weather had turned cold again.

"This is a surprise," I said as I led her inside. "How did you get my address?"

"From Teacher Zhang. He wanted somebody to bring you a message about a meeting at school tomorrow, and I volunteered. You haven't been to school for days. I wondered if you were sick or something." She gave me her shy smile and fidgeted with the fringe of her scarf as if expecting a reproach.

I gave her a glass of hot water to warm her up.

"You're sewing?" she said when she saw the patterns and cloth spread all over the bed and table.

"Uh-huh." I smiled and nodded.

"You can sew? Did you make all these? Did your mom teach you how?"

I laughed. "No one taught me." I showed her the instruction book that I had found in a bookstore. "I learned from here. I just make a paper pattern, and when it looks right I pin it to the cloth and cut."

"That's great! I tried to learn once, but I just couldn't do it. I tried so hard to make a dress, but in the end I had to ask my mother to finish it for me."

My shoulders were aching from bending over the sewing machine all day, and I swung my arms back and forth to relax them. "If you had to do it, you'd learn." I meant what I said. If Lin-lin's family had to live on just sixty yuan a month, and half of their clothes had been confiscated, she would learn to sew too.

She blinked her eyes and changed the subject. "Why haven't you come to school all this time?"

"My mom's been sick."

"Is it serious?"

"Yes. She has Ménière's syndrome. Sometimes she gets so dizzy that she passes out."

"My mother has intestinal angina. When she gets an attack, her belly hurts so much that she rolls around on her bed."

Before I could answer, Ji-yong walked in, with Grandma following him eagerly.

"How was it? Did you see your dad?" Grandma did not even notice our presence.

Ji-yong gloomily shook his head. "In the reception room they were packing apples to sell to the staff, and I asked them if I could buy some for Dad. One of them said, 'Buy apples for your father? You think he's in the hospital or something?' and they all laughed. I'm never going back there."

I looked at Lin-lin with embarrassment. She immediately stood up and said, "It's late. I'd better be going."

I went downstairs to see her off. Neither of us spoke.

"Thanks for coming." I opened the door for her.

"Oh, I almost forgot. Here is your math exercise

notebook. I put the assignment sheet in it. Don't forget the meeting tomorrow. Four o'clock in the auditorium."

My hand was still on the doorknob. Suddenly, without thinking, I said, "My dad has been detained for interrogation."

I surprised myself when I said it. I had not meant to tell her, and I did not know why I trusted her so much after such a short time.

We looked at each other for a while. Finally she said softly, "I understand. Our house was searched too."

She turned and walked away. I watched her doll-like figure retreating through the cold wind, and somehow I felt much warmer.

The meeting had already begun when I arrived at the auditorium. I sat down right by the door. The leader of the school Revolutionary Committee, Chairman Jin, was making a speech on the current revolutionary situation. On the stage beside him were Teacher Hou, a Revolutionary Committee member, and, to my surprise, Chang Hong.

What sort of meeting was this? I looked around to see who was there. There were several Red Guard Committee members and key people from the propaganda group, along with several members of the

Revolutionary Performance Team and the Mao Ze-dong Thought Study Group. Bai Shan was sitting near the door, bending over the paper in his lap.

Was this about the propaganda group again? I had told Chang Hong once already that I wouldn't join. No, that would not require such a formal meeting. While I was still guessing, Chairman Jin finished his summary of the steadily improving revolutionary situation.

"Comrades." He suddenly raised the pitch of his voice. "In order to support the Cultural Revolution and promote class struggle, our school's Red Guard Committee has decided to make a Class Education Exhibition to expose the class enemies' evil and remind us of the misery of the old society and our happiness today. This will inspire our students' revolutionary enthusiasm and further promote the Cultural Revolution in our school.

"Every student here today was handpicked for both academic and political excellence. You will represent all the teachers and students of our school when we celebrate the Communist Party Birthday on July first. . . ."

Academic and political excellence? There must have been a mistake. Even though my classmates didn't know me very well, the teachers certainly knew about my family background. My personal file recorded everything. I imagined the sneers. "Political excellence? A black whelp criticizing landlords?"

In the middle of Chang Hong's speech on behalf of the Red Guard Committee, I slipped unnoticed out of the auditorium and headed for Teacher Zhang's office.

The stairway in the old office building was dark and narrow. At a landing I almost bumped into someone coming down. It was Teacher Zhang himself.

"Teacher Zhang," I stammered, caught unprepared. "I . . . I was coming to see you."

"Oh? Is there something I can help you with? Would you like to come to my office?"

"That's all right. It won't take long." I swallowed and calmed down a little. "I was told to attend the meeting about the exhibition. Did you know that?" I started cautiously.

"I was the one who suggested your name. Did you go? How was it?" he asked lightly.

"Oh. The meeting was fine, but . . . but . . ." I struggled to find the appropriate words. "But I'm not really a leader, am I?" I shook my head slightly and tried to smile.

He didn't answer my question. "I was told you were in the Children's Arts Troupe. Is that true?"

"Um . . ."

"Your Mandarin is excellent, and you won several speech contests. Is that right?"

"Well, that was in primary school, a long time ago.... How did you know?" I felt like he was cornering me.

"I think you're the perfect one to represent our class as a guide at the exhibition."

"Oh, no, no!" I blurted out. My own grandfather was a landlord. How could I condemn the evil landlords of the old society? What if Yin Lan-lan or Du Hai saw me?

"Teacher Zhang, I'm sure there's someone in our class who can do a better job. You'd better find someone else."

"I've thought it over. I think you are the best one. Jiang Ji-li, this is an important political assignment. I hope you will accept it and try to win honor for our class. All right?"

I almost lost the courage to refuse again, but I thought of my landlord grandfather, of Dad detained at the theater.

"Teacher Zhang, did . . . did you ever look at my file?" It took an effort to ask the question. If he knew about the speech contests, then he must know about Grandpa and about the Red Guards searching our apartment.

His face was expressionless as he moved his hand from the railing and put it in his pocket. He did not reply immediately.

"We cannot choose our families or our class status. But we can choose our own futures." He spoke very slowly and clearly. "No, you are not a leader, but you are still an 'educable child.' You can overcome your family background." He paused. "You have self-esteem, and you always try to excel. That's why I believe you are brave enough to face and eventually overcome the difficulties of life."

It was very dark on the stairs. Everything appeared dim except for his piercing, shining eyes. I felt an older brother's sincerity and trust in his look. "'Brave enough to face and eventually overcome the difficulties of life,'" I repeated to myself, and felt something catch in my throat.

"I'll do it," I said simply, and walked away. I was afraid I would cry if I said another word.

The sun was setting, and the western sky was a sheet of gold and rose. I stopped, my heart full of awe at the immensity of the world.

I had wanted to give up. I had almost stopped trying to be brave, to be an educable child. I saw another part of myself, a part full of fear that I had to struggle against. I would not allow myself to stop trying to follow Chairman Mao. Whatever my family background was, I would overcome all difficulties. My future would be bright.

As it grew dark, the whole city seemed to slow down. The school, too, was no longer its bustling daytime self. Only the propaganda group office was ablaze with light, like a brightly lit cabin in the middle of a dark and silent forest.

On the other side of the room Bai Shan and some other boys were painting a picture in preparation for the Class Education Exhibition. We girls were sitting around a big table, gluing dyed millet grains onto a huge sheet of paper to make a portrait of Chairman Mao.

"It's taken us six hours just to finish two eyebrows and the ears. This is going to be a long job!" a girl said. She spoke quickly and loudly, sounding just like her nickname, Ducky.

"If I'd known that it was going to take this long, I would have said let's just draw something," Fang Fang grumbled.

"Come on, we all agreed to do this." Chang Hong moved quickly to put down the disagreement. She pointed at Ducky with her tweezers. "You said that we should do something new and different." She turned to Fang Fang. "And *you* said that the three-dimensional millet grains would look better and show our loyalty to Chairman Mao better than a drawing. Do you remember?"

"I didn't say I wanted to quit. I just said it's slow," Ducky said sulkily.

"We'd better stop arguing and get back to work," I said. "Otherwise we'll never finish." I looked up at the boys' table and hoped that they were not laughing at our squabbling.

"Let's take a break," Chang Hong suggested. "Have some steamed buns while I go make some tea. If we just march on resolutely, we are bound to succeed." She threw a bag of buns on the table and ran out.

No one said anything. Ducky took a bun and bit into it.

That afternoon we couldn't wait to start. We had all bustled around boiling water and dying millet and getting snacks. The enthusiasm had reminded me of the glorious revolutionary activities that I had seen in the movies. We were proud to be part of the revolution, excited to be doing such an important job. Now, only a few hours later, the enthusiasm had completely disappeared. We had not anticipated that the job would take so long. Now it seemed that we would have to work all night to finish before tomorrow's meeting.

I couldn't help yawning. This would be the fourth time I had worked all night since we had started to prepare the exhibition. Although it was months away, there were so many things to do, so many deadlines to meet: deciding on the contents of the exhibition, writing the script, designing the layout, decorating the exhibition hall . . . I was amazed at how I could do so much and still leave time for study and housework.

"Jiang Ji-li," one of the boys called me. I was surprised to find that it was Bai Shan. It was the first time that I had ever heard him call me by name. "The painting is done. When Chang Hong comes back, tell her we've gone home." He started to go, then stopped and gestured toward the painting. "Don't touch it. It's not dry yet."

As soon as the boys left, we rushed to look at their picture. It was a Chinese ink painting. The rising sun was spreading its rays and a rooster was crowing loudly and joyfully.

" 'The Rooster Sings, for the East Is Turning Red,' " Ducky read loudly. "Wow, what a great picture!"

"And the handwriting is so beautiful too," I added. "Bai Shan is really talented, isn't he? He does everything so well."

"You like him, don't you, Ji-li? I think he likes you too. He's always looking at you," Ducky said suddenly.

"Don't be so childish," I snapped. Having my name connected with a boy's was the last thing I needed. Things were hard enough as it was. "Spare me your dirty gossip, all right?"

Just in time, Chang Hong came rushing in. "Here's the tea. What's up? Oh, they're finished? Let me have a look." She elbowed her way to the front.

"What do you think? It's really wonderful, isn't it?" Ducky gushed.

"Hmm . . ." Chang Hong considered. "Why isn't the sun painted red? Since the title is 'The Rooster Sings, for the East Is Turning Red,' the sun should be red, shouldn't it?" Her hand was almost touching the painting.

Ever since Bai Shan had left self-study class that day, Chang Hong had seemed to disapprove of him. She was, after all, a Red Guard Committee member, and she suspected him of disrespect toward Chairman Mao.

I gently moved her hand away. "This is an ink painting. It only uses black ink."

By three o'clock in the morning we could hardly stay awake. Tea and snacks could no longer stimulate our exhausted minds. We yawned in turn, as if we were counting off in formation. As soon as Chang Hong suggested that we take turns sleeping, Ducky and Fang Fang leaned their heads on the table and fell fast asleep. Chang Hong and I washed our faces in cold water and soldiered on toward Chairman Mao's collar.

Outside our office the world seemed to disappear. The dark silence seemed to gradually thicken, until even time could not move as usual. Each minute seemed endless. My eyes were dry and heavy, and I could not control my hands. I had to try over and over to pick up each grain of millet. I wished I could go home to sleep under my own warm quilt.

Home . . . I sighed.

There was still no news about Dad. Mom had secretly asked Uncle Tian for information, but all we knew was that Dad still refused to confess and had been the victim of several struggle meetings. I could not think of those meetings without thinking of the scene-shop foreman's icy stare. I could not help wondering what Dad had done.

I sighed again.

"What's the matter?" Chang Hong raised her sleepy eyes.

"Oh, I'm just sleepy I guess."

A moment later Chang Hong said to me softly, "Ji-li, I envy you so much."

"Envy me? Why?" I was surprised beyond politeness.

"You're so good in school, and so talented—"

"Oh, that doesn't mean anything." Looking into her earnest eyes, I blurted out, "I envy *you*. You have such a good family, and such a good political status."

She looked down at the table blankly. After a long while she spoke again, slowly and softly. "My brother has epilepsy. He's eleven, but he can't dress himself or feed himself." She paused. "He has seizures every day, at least one or two, sometimes more."

"That's terrible!" I could say nothing more.

"I love him very much." She raised her eyes again to look at me. "I'm his favorite. Sometimes he won't eat when my mother tries to feed him, but if I do it, he will."

I could hardly believe that this person was the revolutionary Chang Hong I knew.

"Will he . . . will he die?" I could not stop myself from asking.

She looked down at the table again. It seemed like a long time before she answered. "The doctors say he won't live past his teens. We just don't know. He's not in very good shape these days."

"Why don't you stay home with him? In case . . ."

"I've thought about that." She looked away from my face to the litter on the table. "But we can't allow personal matters to interfere with revolutionary duties. Especially for an important political assignment like the exhibition."

Watching her sincere and earnest eyes, I completely forgot that she was a Red Guard Committee member. Through the quiet of the early morning we talked and talked, like friends or sisters.

By the time our classmates arrived at school the next morning, we had finally completed the picture—made with thousands of millet grains and thousands of yawns. But we could not enjoy our accomplishment or the praise of teachers and classmates. We put our heads on the table and fell fast asleep.

HALF-CITY JIANGS

Finally, one May evening, Uncle Tian brought us some thrilling news: Dad was cleared of the charge of listening to foreign radio.

It turned out that Uncle Zhu—not Uncle Fan—was to blame. Uncle Zhu had been detained himself, and had wanted to improve his own situation by cooperating with the investigation. He had made up the story about the foreign radio, thinking that if he confessed to something, he would be treated with leniency. When Dad steadily denied his participation, the theater people got angrier and angrier. They pressed Uncle Zhu for details. He stupidly told them that he and Dad had used a transistor radio, which they had buried in Zhu's courtyard. The theater people went straight to Zhu's house and tore up the courtyard looking for the evidence, but they found nothing. They were furious and gave Uncle Zhu a good beating. Finally he admitted to making up the whole story.

What a terrible man, I thought, worse than a traitor. At least a traitor betrays people by telling the truth. Uncle Zhu tried to save himself by telling lies.

We were all overjoyed that Dad would be coming home. Grandma was in tears, and she could not stop thanking Allah for his blessing. Mom seemed much better, and Ji-yun kept pestering Grandma to buy shrimp, Dad's favorite food, for his homecoming. For the first time in my life I thought maybe there really was a God who had heard the prayers Grandma had been saying every night since Dad had been detained.

I had the window over the sink open, and warm air blew over my face as I rinsed the vegetables and put the rice on the stove.

I heard steps on the stairs, and thought it was Mom coming back from the doctor. But when I turned around I saw Dad. I shouted. Grandma and Ji-yun came running out the door. As we met on the landing, Dad lifted his arms to embrace us. Then he immediately lowered them and glanced over his shoulder at the two stern men who were right behind him. Ji-yong pounded up the stairs and pushed between the men, then stopped.

"I came . . . to get some clothes," Dad said.

"Aren't you coming back to stay?" Ji-yong asked,

and we all looked at Dad. He just shook his head.

"We're going to have shrimp," Ji-yun announced hopefully.

Grandma started to say something, then looked at Dad's two escorts and shut her mouth. She hurried away to open the chest, and the rest of us followed Dad slowly into the apartment. Even Ji-yun was silent now.

It had been three months since I had seen him last. He looked smaller. His old blue jacket hung loosely on his body, and his back stooped wearily. His shaggy hair hung over his collar, and the black stubble on his face made his eyes seem even more sunken.

We all looked at each other, wanting to ask so many questions but not daring to say anything in front of the guards. Grandma hurried up and laid a pile of clothes on the table. Her hands shook, and so did Dad's as he took the bag she handed him. He slowly sorted through the clothes and put some of them in his bag.

Something wet fell on the bag.

I looked up. A tear rolled down Dad's cheek, and another. He wiped it away, but as soon as he did, another took its place.

I had never seen Dad cry before. Soon I was crying too, and so was Ji-yun. We all wept along with him.

"Let's go. Bring your clothes," one of the men ordered.

Dad picked up his bag and looked at us. "I'm going. Be good. Tell your mother to take care of herself." He turned toward Grandma but then turned his eyes away. "Good-bye, Mother." He quickly followed the two men down the stairs.

We clung to each other as we watched him go. We all dashed up to the roof to watch him walk down the alley. He walked a little in front of his escorts. The triangle made by the three heads grew smaller and smaller.

"Dad!" Ji-yun finally shouted, but he had already vanished around the corner.

A week passed and Dad still had not come home. And no one knew why.

As I came up the stairs after school, Mom was just seeing a man and a woman out the door. I had never seen them before, and I immediately wondered if they had come with news about Dad. Leaning weakly on the doorframe, Mom politely said, "Please take care," several times, but the visitors went straight downstairs without making any response.

I walked into the room and saw two cups of tea on the table, no longer hot but obviously untouched.

Grandma had collapsed in the old rattan chair, not moving, her face pale and filled with despair. Mom sat down and leaned limply against the back of her chair. Her eyes were closed and she said nothing. I could not bring myself to ask what had happened. I fiddled with the cold teacups, more and more nervous.

After a long while Mom gestured for me to sit down beside her.

"Yesterday's *Workers' Revolt* had an article on the front page about the Jiang family." She had to stop for breath. "It said that the Jiangs were a big landlord family in Nanjing that owned over thirty-three hundred acres of land and lots of businesses. They were so rich that people called them the 'Half-City Jiangs.' Would you go buy a paper? I want to look at it."

I blinked my eyes in confusion but could not get up.

Mom nodded in the direction of the untouched teacups on the table. "The people who were just here came to investigate. Your cousins were mentioned in the article, and they wanted to know more about them. . . ."

I did not hear the rest of what Mom was saying. My mind was swimming. "Half-City Jiangs" and "thirty-three hundred acres of land"! Everybody read the

Workers' Revolt. Suddenly I pictured my teachers and classmates reading the sensational article, passing it around and gossiping about it. "Jiang Ji-li's family is the Half-City Jiangs . . . thirty-three hundred acres of land." Somehow I found myself standing up, a teacup in my hand, and a puddle of spilled tea on the table.

Why had my parents hidden these things from me? What else was there? Had Dad really committed a crime? Why hadn't the theater let him come home? Anger rose in me. Didn't they know how hard I'd been working to overcome my family background? Now all my efforts were wasted.

"I hate landlords. I hate this landlord family," I burst out. They were the first words I had spoken since I got home.

As I turned to leave, I saw tears welling out of Mom's closed eyes.

I had not talked to Mom for two days. If she asked me to help set the table or to call Ji-yong to dinner, I did it, but I did not say a word to her. Every time I looked at her, I saw the tears welling out of her eyes, but I could not apologize.

As usual, I walked past the police station on the way home from school. When I was past it and almost to the corner, I stopped. I hesitated for a long time, then turned back.

It was lunchtime. There was no one in the street in front of the police station. The red light beside the gate seemed to welcome me.

I timidly looked inside. The room was so dark that I could not see whether anyone was there or not. I started to turn away. I could come back another time, I told myself.

I heard Pudge's snide voice again. *"Jiang Ji-li, is your family related to Chiang Kai-shek too?"* My other classmates had stood in excited knots, looking at me over their shoulders, before turning back to their gossip. I remembered the jeering chant of the neighborhood boys who had followed me down the alley: *"Half-City Jiangs! Half-City Jiangs! Down with the landlord Half-City Jiangs!"*

No! I did not want to have this damned name anymore! I had had enough. All my bad luck and humiliation came from the name Jiang. I had seen stories in the paper about people who had changed their names. They had started life anew. If I just dropped my family name, I could be named Ji Li and be lucky, just as it meant.

I stepped forward. "Comrade?" I called toward the dark reception room. No one answered.

I looked at the directory and headed up the stairs to the household registration office.

The sign on the door said, RESIDENCE REGISTRATION, and below that was an even larger sign that said, NO ENTRANCE WITHOUT PERMISSION. There was a barred window about two feet square and a huge slogan, which occupied one whole wall: CLASS STRUGGLE IS THE KEY.

I looked through the window. The office was empty, but the lights were on, and I could hear a radio playing behind a plywood partition.

"Comrade."

There was no answer.

"Comrade?" I raised my voice and knocked loudly on the counter.

A chair moved inside the office, and a man came out from behind the plywood partition. It was Officer Ma, the policeman in charge of residence registration for our neighborhood.

"What do you want?" he asked impatiently before he even looked at me. "Can't you let me have lunch in peace?" He waved his chopsticks at me.

"I'm sorry. I'm sorry. I'm terribly sorry," I said, shrinking back with my schoolbag in front of me like a shield.

"What is it?" He stared down at me through the window, picking his teeth with his finger.

"I can wait until you've finished lunch," I said apologetically.

"I asked you what you want, but I don't care if you don't want to tell me." He turned around.

"Wait! I . . . I want to change my name," I said timidly.

"What?"

"I want to change my name."

"Change your name? Why?" He picked his teeth again.

"I . . . I don't have a good class status. So I want to change my family name."

He took his finger out of his mouth and began to pay attention. "Good. Revolutionary action." He opened the door. "Come in, come in. I'll be ready in no time."

I looked at him nervously. When he came into our alley, he held his head high and spoke in domineering tones. He seemed to swagger, and enjoyed having power. I did not trust this sudden friendliness.

He pointed me to a chair. "Making a clean break with your black family, that's good. We absolutely support you."

Break with my family? I did not understand him.

"Chairman Mao says you can't choose your class status but you can choose your future. You couldn't choose the family you were born into, but now that you've grown up, it's time for you to choose your future. You can tell your parents you'll follow Chairman Mao, not them. If they give you any trouble, just come here and tell us. We'll go to their work units and hold struggle meetings against them. . . ."

He went on and on, waving his chopsticks. I was totally confused. I had only wanted to break with all those landlords in my family, not with Mom and Dad. Would changing my name mean breaking off relations with them? I thought of Aunt Xi-wen lying in the alley, and Shan-shan walking right past her.

"Well, I'll go wash my hands and be back to register you in a minute." He walked out of the office.

I sat in the empty room, picturing telling Mom and Dad that I had changed my name.

I jumped up and ran out.

The street was still the same. The sun was shining warmly, and there were few people in sight. I slowly loosened my fist from the strap of my schoolbag. It was dripping with sweat.

★　★　★

I was still sweating as I walked in our back door. On the stairs I could hear Grandma talking to someone.

"Please don't. You shouldn't do that. Please."

I stopped and listened.

"Please give me the mop. When you do this, it makes us feel guilty." Grandma's voice was anxious now.

I knew who she was talking to then. Song Po-po must have come to mop the stairs. Ever since Dad had been detained, she had been doing things for us again. When we were not watching, she came and mopped the stairs. Every few days she bought some vegetables for us, and sometimes she even washed them and chopped them. Grandma tried to stop her, but Song Po-po would not listen.

"Mrs. Jiang, don't worry. It's nothing, I just do it when I don't have anything to do. I did it for so long, I just can't get used to not doing it. Besides, you're having hard times right now and you need help. Don't worry, I won't let anybody see me."

It sounded like Grandma went into the apartment. I was sure Song Po-po had gone back to her mopping.

Suddenly I found myself weeping. What everyone else was saying about us did not make any difference to Song Po-po. She treated us just the way she always used to. Life couldn't be easy for her either, since she no longer had a job, but she was still concerned about others. I felt ashamed. I had been selfish and inconsiderate. Life was difficult for me, but it was even more difficult for Mom. How could I think of hurting her this way?

I heard Song Po-po go back into her room. I ran in and gave her a hug.

"Be careful, child, be careful. I'm just bringing this bowl of soup to your mother."

"I'll take it," I said.

THE CLASS EDUCATION EXHIBITION

The mournful sound of a Chinese fiddle echoed around the booths in the school exhibition hall.

It's only a preview, I thought. I was a veteran of many speech contests and I should not have been so nervous. But the school leaders and district leaders were coming to evaluate us, and because of that article in the *Workers' Revolt*, the preview became especially important to me.

The article had been like a bomb blowing holes in my life. In our alley, at school, and at Mom's office people gossiped about our family. I had thought I was going to be kicked out of the exhibition. Each night as I lay in bed, I told myself that I would rather quit than be rejected; I would talk to Chang Hong the next day. Then each day in school I had been seized by a new determination not to give in to pressure. I knew that I could represent the class better than anyone else. Why should I quit? Why let those old landlords ruin my life?

Finally I had decided. Everyone already knew the worst about me. Let them think what they would. I would do an excellent job to prove myself. I had to win my honor back.

The exhibition hall seemed like a new building. The partitions between the cafeteria and the gym had been taken down, and the space had been redivided into twelve booths. The pictures, photos, drawings, and clay statues displayed in each booth gave the hall a strong serious atmosphere. I was narrating the part on the horrors of the old China.

"Now let's look at two more of Liu Wen-cai's slaves," I said, gesturing to the statues of the infamous landlord and his victims.

"This is the blind old grandfather. Every day, in bitter cold or in scorching sun, his little granddaughter led him out to beg for their food. With the little food that he managed to receive, how could he repay his debt to the landlord? Each year the debt increased. Finally, Liu Wen-cai forced him to give his granddaughter in payment. How could he do that? She was his eyes, his whole life. But what else could he do to escape from this brutal landlord? With tears in his sightless eyes, he said to her, 'My dearest, you must go with Mr. Liu. It is not because I do not love you, it is

that black-hearted landlord who is tearing us apart.'"
My voice trembled slightly, and I became more and
more emotional as I spoke.

"The poor granddaughter had never been separated
from her grandfather before. He was the one who
tucked her quilt around her each night, and he was the
one who comforted her when she cried." I pointed to
the statues. "Look at her, crying piteously as she is
pulled away by the landlord, her hand stretching out to
her grandfather. . . ."

I was nearly in tears as I finished my presentation.
Dozens of evaluators were wiping their eyes as Teacher
Yu moved them on to the next booth. Even Bai Shan,
who was in charge of the exhibit's design and had heard
my presentation several times in rehearsal, was blinking
back tears.

I heaved a long sigh and collapsed onto my stool. I
wiped my sweaty hands on my pants and picked up a
book to fan myself.

"Ji-li." I heard someone outside the window calling me. I raised the bamboo blind and saw An Yi and
Lin-lin.

"What are you doing here?"

"We wanted to see your presentation, but they
wouldn't let us in. We had to stand here and listen to

you. You did a terrific job!" An Yi's face was glowing.

"It's true. You were very good." Lin-lin was more reserved but just as sincere.

"Well, it's such a touching story that anyone could make it work." I leaned farther out the window.

Someone patted me on the back.

"What are you doing? Get in here! Chairman Jin is coming."

Hastily I drew back inside. The visitors who had just left were standing in front of me again. Chang Hong whispered to me, "Chairman Jin wants to talk to you."

I shivered. I knew this would happen, I thought. Now he was going to say I was a landlord's granddaughter, and humiliate me in front of everyone. I should have quit after all. I should have— I was so flustered that I knocked over a stool as I approached Chairman Jin.

Chairman Jin towered over me. I looked up into his serious eyes and immediately lowered mine.

"This Class Education Exhibition is a very powerful weapon," he said. "Appropriately used, it can strengthen class identification and deepen the hatred of class enemies. Your presentation was very emotional, and the audience was deeply affected. I hope you can help the others to improve their presentations, and make the exhibition a success."

I was puzzled. Was he praising me? I looked around the group and saw nothing but approval in their eyes.

"By the way, I suggest you add a quotation from Chairman Mao's works to the end of the presentation, so you can finish on an inspiring note." Chairman Jin clasped his hands behind his back and looked at the others as if he were asking for their opinions. Everyone nodded. Chang Hong was taking notes with a proud smile on her face.

They went on to another booth to make their suggestions. I slowly sat down, shouting to myself, "I did it!"

During Math class a few days later, Teacher Hou from the Revolutionary Committee popped his head into my classroom. He barely glanced at Teacher Li before saying curtly, "Jiang Ji-li, come to our office right away. Someone wants to talk to you."

I stood up nervously, wondering what it could be. I felt my classmates' piercing eyes as I mechanically left the classroom. Teacher Hou walked ahead of me without seeming to notice my presence. I followed silently.

I tried not to panic. Maybe it was not bad.

Maybe it was about the exhibition. Maybe Chairman Jin wanted me to help the others with their presentations. At the end of the long, dark hallway Teacher Hou silently motioned me into the office and then walked away.

I wiped my hands on my trousers and slowly opened the door. The thin-faced foreman from Dad's theater was right in front of me.

My face must have shown my dismay.

"Sit down, sit down. Don't be afraid." Chairman Jin pointed to the empty chair. "These comrades from your father's work unit are just here to have a study session with you. It's nothing to worry about."

I sat down dumbly.

I had thought about their coming to my home but never imagined this. They were going to expose my family in front of my teachers and classmates. I would have no pride left. I would never be an educable child again.

Thin-Face sat opposite me, with a woman I had never seen before. Teacher Zhang was there too, his eyes encouraging me.

Thin-Face came straight to the point. "Your father's problems are very serious." His cold eyes nailed me to my seat. "You may have read the article in the *Workers'*

Revolt that exposed your family's filthy past." I slumped down in my chair without taking my eyes off his face. "In addition to coming from a landlord family, your father committed some serious mistakes during the Antirightist Movement several years ago, but he still obstinately refuses to confess." His cold manner became a little more animated. "Of course we won't tolerate this. We have decided to make an example of him. We are going to have a struggle meeting of the entire theater system to criticize him and force him to confess." He suddenly pounded the table with his fist. The cups on the table rattled.

I tore my eyes away from him and stared at a cup instead.

"As I told you before, you are your own person. If you want to make a clean break with your black family, then you can be an educable child and we will welcome you to our revolutionary ranks." He gave Chairman Jin a look, and Chairman Jin chimed in, "That's right, we welcome you."

"Jiang Ji-li has always done well at school. In addition to doing very well in her studies, she participates in educational reform," Teacher Zhang added.

"That's very good. We knew that you had more sense than to follow your father," Thin-Face said with a brief, frozen smile. "Now you can show your revolutionary determination." He paused. "We want you to testify against your father at the struggle meeting."

I closed my eyes. I saw Dad standing on a stage, his head bowed, his name written in large black letters, and then crossed out in red ink, on a sign hanging from his neck. I saw myself standing in the middle of the stage, facing thousands of people, condemning Dad for his crimes, raising my fist to lead the chant, "Down with Jiang Xi-reng." I saw Dad looking at me hopelessly, tears on his face.

"I . . . I . . ." I looked at Teacher Zhang for help. He looked away.

The woman from the theater spoke. "It's really not such a hard thing to do. The key is your class stance. The daughter of our former Party Secretary resolved to make a clean break with her mother. When she went onstage to condemn her mother, she actually slapped her face. Of course, we don't mean that you have to slap your father's face. The point is that as long as you have the correct class stance, it will be easy to testify." Her voice grated on my ears.

"There is something you can do to prove you are truly Chairman Mao's child." Thin-Face spoke again. "I am sure you can tell us some things your father said and did that show his landlord and rightist mentality." I stared at the table, but I could feel his eyes boring into me. "What can you tell us?"

"But I don't know anything," I whispered. "I don't know—"

"I am sure you can remember something if you think about it," Thin-Face said. "A man like him could not hide his true beliefs from a child as smart as you. He must have made comments critical of Chairman Mao and the Cultural Revolution. I am sure you are loyal to Chairman Mao and the Communist Party. Tell us!"

"But my father never said anything against Chairman Mao," I protested weakly. "I would tell you if he did." My voice grew stronger with conviction. "He never said anything against the Party."

"Now, you have to choose between two roads." Thin-Face looked straight into my eyes. "You can break with your family and follow Chairman Mao, or you can follow your father and become an enemy of the people." His voice grew more severe. "In that case we would have many more study sessions, with your brother and sister too, and the Red Guard Committee and the school leaders. Think about it. We will come back to talk to you again."

Thin-Face and the woman left, saying they would

be back to get my statement. Without knowing how I got there, I found myself in a narrow passageway between the school building and the school-yard wall. The gray concrete walls closed around me, and a slow drizzle dampened my cheeks. I could not go back to the classroom, and I could not go home. I felt like a small animal that had fallen into a trap, alone and helpless, and sure that the hunter was coming.

All night I hardly slept. I saw Thin-Face's hard eyes, and I saw tears on Dad's cheeks. In the early morning I finally fell into a troubled sleep. I awoke just half an hour before I had to report to the exhibition. I washed and dressed and ran out the door, still rubbing my swollen eyes.

I pushed yesterday's events out of my mind. Today was the opening of the exhibition, and I was determined to do a good job.

I approached the exhibition hall. Through the open door I could see everyone sitting in a circle. The briefing had already started. I broke into a run. Someone stepped toward me from the shadow of the holly bush beside the door: Bai Shan.

I knew he had been taking an interest in me, but I had never showed I noticed. I did not want to be gossiped about. I ran by, wondering what he was doing there.

"Jiang Ji-li," he said softly. "Brace yourself."

I paused, but I was already inside. Chairman Jin looked up at me. Following his eyes, all the students turned toward me as well. Chairman Jin stared at me, and I stopped, rooted to the floor. For an eternity I was surrounded by a deafening silence.

"Jiang Ji-li," Chairman Jin said at last. "Yesterday we—that is the Revolutionary Committee—discussed your situation. Because of your political situation we decided to let Fang Fang replace you. You can go home now. I'll talk to you later."

His face was cold and closed. I looked at the others, those who had laughed and joked and prepared the presentation with me for months. Some looked sympathetic, and some turned their eyes away. I could not bear to see any more. I ran out of the hall.

"Jiang Ji-li!" I heard someone calling my name, but I just lowered my head and kept running.

"Jiang Ji-li!" Someone passed and stopped in front of me: Bai Shan again.

I turned my eyes away. I struggled to look calm, to keep him from seeing my shame. I did not want his pity.

He looked at me for a few seconds before he spoke. "Here, this is yours." He handed me something. It was dark green. A book. A dictionary, with "Jiang" written in the corner. I had left it in the exhibition booth.

I did not say a word. I did not look at him. I did not take the book. I just ran away.

THE RICE HARVEST

I did not know why Chang Hong wanted to talk with me.

I walked to school in the shade of the buildings. The sun was hot. In the still, heavy air my back was soaked with sweat before I had walked out of the alley. The whole city seemed to have slowed down. The few bicycles that passed seemed to be pedaling slowly through a murky oil. Even the cicadas chirped listlessly.

Three days after I had been thrown out of the exhibition, Chang Hong had sent a message to my home to insist that we meet at the Red Guard Committee office. "It's not convenient to have this conversation at your home or mine," she said. Obviously she had some official statement to pass on to me, but for once I did not care. I did not care about anything but Thin-Face's demands. I had no secrets, no goals, and no need to make any effort to impress anybody. I passed the police station where I had almost changed my name. Idly I wondered if anything would be different now if I had done it. The idea seemed to be just another fantasy, with no more reality than a dream of flying.

The Red Guard Committee office was on the sixth floor, the top floor, of the new building of the school. The doors of a few offices were open, but no voices drifted out of them. Through the hallway window I could see the national flag on its flagpole. In the heat even it was drooping. Its five yellow stars were invisible.

Chang Hong opened the door to my knock. While she poured me a glass of cool water, I looked around the small office. It was full of red: red slogans, red posters, red armbands, and red flags. A huge poster of Chairman Mao in a green army uniform, waving to the Red Guards from the Tienanmen rostrum, covered almost an entire wall. There were posters of Chairman Mao's poems written in his own calligraphy, and a new poster of a group of Red Guards in belted army uniforms poised to march forward, waiting only for the Great Leader's order.

"I've been wanting to have a talk with you for a while, and now it seems even more important," Chang Hong said. We had not really talked for a long time, and I thought she looked a little depressed. How was her brother's epilepsy? I wondered suddenly.

"I was informed that you requested to do your summer labor in the factories instead of the countryside," she went on. "Is that true?"

"Yes. My mother has been quite ill recently, and Grandma is very old. If Mom had to go the hospital, Grandma and my brother and my sister wouldn't be strong enough to take her. That's why I asked to be assigned to a factory in the city this year. That way I'll be able to work and take care of Mom too." I was extraordinarily calm, I thought.

"I know about your family situation." Chang Hong crossed her arms and rested her elbows earnestly on the table. "I know you want to take care of your family. Undoubtedly there are difficulties. But Ji-li, have you considered the importance of your political life? It's not your fault that you were born into such a family, but the class influence of your family does have an effect. This makes your task of remolding yourself harder than other people's. A slight slackening could easily cause you to be recaptured by your family and turned into their follower.

"Chairman Jin told me that your father's work unit spoke to you about breaking with your black family. You hesitated, and that was why he replaced you in the exhibition. But Ji-li, it's not too late. If you go to the countryside to do your summer labor, the sweat of honest work will wash the black stain from your back and purify your mind so that you can follow Chairman Mao's revolutionary line. If you prove you are an educable child, maybe Chairman Jin will put you back in the exhibition for the end of summer.

"This is a crucial moment for you! How could you ask to work in a factory instead? Ji-li, I was really worried for you when I heard that. I wanted to scold you for being so shortsighted. There is no difficulty, no matter how serious, that cannot be overcome, but if you miss this chance, it might ruin your whole political life. Then it will be too late to repent."

Chang Hong finally paused for breath. I could see that she was nearly in tears. She was so sincere, and she had so much faith in me. I was moved deeply by her caring. While other classmates were afraid of being too close to me, she still worried about me, felt sorry for me, and tried to think of what was best for me. I knew that she believed what she said: She wanted to help me, to rescue me from my black family.

"All right, I'll go," I said slowly.

"That's great! I knew you wanted to go forward. You'll thank yourself for taking advantage of this chance to follow Chairman Mao's revolutionary line."

I smiled at her with sincere gratitude. I did not want to disappoint her. I would go and try to prove myself. Maybe what she said was true, maybe they would accept me after I had done summer labor. More likely what she had told me was simply an order from Chairman Jin and I had no choice but to remold myself. No matter what, there was one good thing about going to the countryside. I felt a sudden surge of relief. While I was there, Thin-Face could not come to make me testify against Dad.

"How's your brother?" I patted her arm and changed the subject.

As agreed, I went off with my classmates, resolved to do my share of the labor that fed us all.

We were sent to help with the "double rush," rush harvesting and rush planting. This was the busiest time of the year for the farmers, when they had to harvest the first crop of rice and immediately plant the second crop.

At five thirty in the morning we got up from our beds—straw mats in a storage room—and went to work harvesting the rice. In the still morning air the rising sun turned the rice field into a golden sea. Each of us was assigned five rows, rows that seemed endless. We bent over the rice and concentrated on what the farmers had told us: Sickle in the right hand, grab six plants with the left hand, cut them at the roots, take one step forward. We slogged ahead.

The sun burned down on us with a force that seemed to press us deeper into the mud. In a few minutes our thick jackets were soaked with sweat. The golden rice field stretched in front of us. We wielded our sickles mechanically, thinking of nothing but finishing our assigned rows. At noon lunch was sent to the rice fields. We gobbled our lunch in a few minutes and rushed back to work. By midafternoon our backs seemed about to break. Some people were forced to kneel in the mud and inch forward. As soon as we finished work, we threw ourselves on our mats and fell fast asleep, oblivious to our sweaty, filthy bodies and crying stomachs.

By the third day we were all exhausted.

I finally reached the low ridge that marked the end of the field and sat down. Another row finished! I closed my eyes. Every muscle, every joint in my body was aching. I wondered if the arthritis I had suffered as a child was returning. To force that thought out of my mind, I opened my eyes and took the towel from my neck to wipe my face. The stench of stale sweat on the cloth almost made me sick.

I slowly straightened my back and looked at the girl next to me. She had finished four rows and was already working on her fifth! I had done only three. I looked at the sun, already close to the horizon. It was probably five o'clock. Yesterday I had finished my fifth row in the darkness after everyone else had left the fields. I was even slower today. I felt a rush of alarm and picked up my sickle. I ran to the next row and began to cut frantically.

"Six plants, cut! Six plants, cut!" I repeated to myself, straining to make my arms and legs perform. Suddenly the sickle slipped out of my exhausted hand, and a two-inch gash appeared on my leg. Blood oozed out of the cut. I covered it with my muddy hand and cried with pain and frustration.

A weak breeze rustled the rice plants, and I could almost hear them talking to me. I raised my head. There was no one near me. No one would hear me crying. No one would come help me. It was getting dark, but no matter what, I still had to finish the five rows. Otherwise I would be disgraced. I stopped crying and took the towel off my neck to bind the wound.

It hurt badly. I clenched my teeth and took up the sickle again, forcing myself to think only of finishing the job. The pain slowly dulled.

Suddenly I heard something. I stopped cutting. A regular *swish, swish, swish* was moving in my direction. It did not sound like the wind rustling the grain. I looked around the field and saw no one; all the others had finished. The field was dark. I thought of how far I was from any house or any person, and my heart raced. *Swish, swish, swish.* I felt my legs growing weaker and weaker. If someone attacked me I would never be able to fight him off. I sank to my knees, holding my sickle in my trembling hand, and waited.

The sound stopped, and someone stood up from the paddy. It was Bai Shan.

He put down the rice in his hand and straightened to ease his back. He was about to bend over again when he saw me rise. We stood about twenty yards apart and stared at each other.

"It's getting dark. I'm helping you cut a little." He smiled apologetically. His voice was low but clear in the quiet of the open field. Against the dusky sky he looked like a statue, tall and strong. I suddenly started to cry.

"Why are you crying?" He ran to my side. "Don't . . . don't cry. I'll help you. We'll finish in no time." His voice was affectionate but also flustered, like that of a child who had no idea what to do.

I only cried harder. I felt as if I were pouring out the whole year's grievances.

"Come on, you." He saw me wiping my tears with my muddy hands and held his own towel up to my face. "Just stop crying and take a break. I'll finish for you." Mumbling, he bent over and began to cut.

I cried and cried. Then a thought struck me. What was I doing? I was letting a boy help me. I did not need his pity. And if anyone found out, I would be criticized, and he would get in trouble too. I stopped crying and picked up my sickle. I walked over to his side and put my foot in front of the rice he was going to cut.

"Let me do it myself," I said.

"That's okay. I don't have anything else to do. Besides, I'm faster than you, and you'll get to go back sooner."

"No. What if somebody sees us?"

"It's dark. They won't see." He tried to nudge me out of the way.

I did not move.

"I said I don't want your help!" My voice was cold and stubborn.

He stood up. A clump of rice was still dangling from his left hand. His eyes were full of confusion, sympathy, and disappointment.

Everything was dark. His tall figure dissolved into the night, but I could still feel his eyes on me, shining despite the darkness.

I felt something new and unsettling, something I could not understand. I lowered my head and nervously said, "Please leave me alone."

When I looked up again, he had already vanished.

Early in the morning the work bell rang. I rubbed my sleepy eyes and looked out. Another sunny day. We would not get a day off after all. And last night after dinner we had threshed until midnight because the forecast had been for rain.

I moved my body a little and almost groaned out loud. My head felt as if it were going to split, and my throat was swollen and sore. Every muscle in my body ached. The day before, I had started to feel sick, and I was sure I was coming down with a fever. I painfully turned over and closed my eyes.

Almost immediately I jerked myself upright. I could not go back to sleep. I had determined to face the challenge of the double rush, to remold myself, and I had to succeed. I had to go to work.

I struggled to my feet, took two of the painkiller

pills I had brought with me, and trudged toward the threshing ground.

Bai Shan was there already, hard at work. I walked quickly to the thresher farthest from his and picked up a bundle of rice.

I held bundle after bundle into the mouth of the thresher and turned them over and over against a whirling drum to strip all the ripe kernels from the straw. Grains of rice jumped out of the machine and stung my face so often that in no time my whole face felt numb. The sun seemed determined to melt us. In a few minutes I was dripping with sweat. I felt as if I were in a huge oven, scorched by the ever-increasing heat.

I thought of popsicles. Four fen apiece, cream, red bean, or lemon-flavored. I imagined holding one in my mouth and feeling each swallow of delicious icy water flow down my throat. I thought of resting in the shade, leisurely fanning myself. I thought of sitting in a tub full of cold water reading a novel.

I tried hard to imagine cool things to distract myself, but my legs began to tremble, and my eyes would not focus. I could not see clearly—not the thresher roller, not the bundle of rice in my hand. "Don't fall down, don't fall down. It will be all right after today," I told myself again and again. I repeated

Chairman Mao's quotation, "Be resolute, fear no sacrifice, and surmount every difficulty to win victory."

Just before noon, when I turned around to get another bundle of rice, I lost consciousness.

I was in an enormous classroom, with a vaulted ceiling like a medieval cathedral. It was packed with people, and I was sitting in the very last row. At some signal I did not see, all the others put on white gowns with hoods that left only two black holes for the eyes. In the thrilling silence they all turned their heads to me. They all moved in perfect unison.

I wanted to shout. I wanted to escape. But I could not move. Then something forced me to stand up and walk step by step up the aisle in the vacuumlike silence. The white hoods and the eyes glinting behind the black holes followed me. . . .

I ran and ran, through an endless and featureless yellow desert. I did not know what I ran from or where I was running to. I staggered, and fell, and crawled. Suddenly an enormous black shadow stood in front of me. I looked up. It was a giant Bai Shan. His hands rested on his hips, and his voice echoed: "Ha, ha, ha, Jiang Ji-li. Ha, ha, ha."

I awoke.

I was lying on my straw mat in the empty storage room, all alone. I stretched. My whole body was sore, and I still felt that unbearable headache. I remembered what had happened in the morning. "Stupid!" I said to myself angrily. It was just luck that I hadn't fallen forward into the machine.

I lay there and basked in the stillness. The rumble of the motors and the noises of the people on the threshing ground were very far away. I was free. No one was watching me, no one was investigating my family. I just lay there, at peace.

"Ji-li." A loud voice jerked me awake. Chang Hong rushed in.

"Chang-Hong! What are you doing here? I thought you were working in a factory. When did you come?" I sat up, surprised and happy to see her.

"I just got here. Teacher Zhang had to go back to a meeting in Shanghai, so I came here to take his place. They told me you fainted this morning, so I came to see you first thing." She threw her traveling bag on the floor and plopped down beside my mat. "Well, feeling better?"

"Much." I smiled gratefully. "I'm sure I can go back to work tomorrow."

"You're not going to work tomorrow. You're going

back to Shanghai tonight." She stopped smiling.

"Not me. I'll never be a quitter."

"You're not a quitter," she said in a softer voice. "Your father's theater wants you to do some study sessions with them. The Revolutionary Committee asked me to tell you." She watched my face as she spoke, then put her hand comfortingly on mine. "Ji-li, don't worry. . . ."

"I know." I cut her off rudely as I lay down again and turned my face away. "You don't need to say anything."

THE INCRIMINATING LETTER

It was good to be home, in spite of my worry about the summons from the theater. I lay in bed, my mind wandering and my body reveling in the softness. Every muscle and every joint in my body ached.

Someone knocked very softly at the door: two knocks, a pause, and three more. Mom opened the door without even asking who was there, and I heard Uncle Tian's voice. He and Mom disappeared into the bathroom.

Before long the bathroom door opened again and Mom showed Uncle Tian out. "I'll let you know when I've finished revising it." She closed the door behind him and came back in. "It's late. Go to sleep," she said to me softly. She put some pieces of paper onto her nightstand and went back into the bathroom.

I turned off the light and closed my eyes. What were those papers? Why had she said, "I'll let you know when it's finished"? What was going on?

It was very quiet in the room. Ji-yong and Ji-yun had fallen asleep a while ago. Grandma was dozing on her bed, with her glasses on her nose and the newspaper on her chest. I heard Mom washing and knew she would be in the bathroom for at least fifteen minutes. Impulsively I slipped out of bed and, without even putting on my slippers, tiptoed over to Mom's bed.

Several sheets of paper were folded together on the nightstand. I picked up the one on top and held it under the soft light of Mom's bedside lamp. I held my breath as I read the first words: "Respected Comrades of the Municipal Party Committee."

I pressed the letter against my chest. The beginning of it made me too nervous to read any further. I heard Mom turning the water tap and looked guiltily over my shoulder. Then I read the rest of the letter as fast as I could.

The letter complained about the situation in the theater. The faction in power, the Rebels, did whatever they wanted, ignoring the policy directives from the Central Committee of the Party, the letter said. They treated people with nonpolitical problems, like Aunt Wu, as class enemies, and they had humiliated her, shaving half of her head in a yin-yang hairdo. They frequently beat their prisoners and had already beaten two to death. They even recorded the screams and moans of the prisoners being tortured, and played the tapes to frighten other prisoners under interrogation.

"We urgently hope," the letter concluded, "that the Municipal Party Committee will investigate this situation and correct it before it is too late." The letter was signed, "The Revolutionary Masses."

I tiptoed back to bed. My heart pounded inside my chest. Although the letter was merely reporting facts to a superior, it was a complaint about the Rebels at the theater. If they found out about it, Mom and Uncle Tian would be in serious trouble. And what would happen to Dad and Aunt Wu? What if Thin-Face found out? Would he blame me for not telling him?

I heard Mom go to bed. Lying in the darkness with my eyes open, I could not stop imagining all the horrors that could result from this letter. I was scared, and I did not know what to do.

It was dusk. I was shelling soybeans. Ji-yun and her classmate Xiao Hong-yin were laughing and chatting in the room and Ji-yong was busy making a slingshot. Running water was gurgling from the roof. Grandma was washing clothes. Mom had gone to answer a telephone call.

The kitchen was getting dark, but I did not bother to turn the light on. I stared out the window. Another day had passed, and still Thin-Face had not shown up. What was he waiting for? What should I say when he came? What would he do to me?

I sighed and shelled more beans.

How was Dad? Surely they must have struggled with him enough. Had they beaten him? Since I had read Mom's letter two days ago, I had seen Dad in my mind, not just carrying concrete pipes and wiping away tears, but being tortured.

Had he really done something wrong? Why wouldn't he confess if he had? Was he really a rightist as they said? . . .

Suddenly pounding feet on the stairs jerked me back to reality. Mom ran up the stairs panic-stricken, yelling, "The letter, the letter." Grandma and I followed Mom into the room.

"The theater people are coming to search the house. The Dictatorship Group is watching the entrance to the alley. They wouldn't even let me answer the phone." We all stared at her as she reached under her pillow. "Quick!" Mom thrust a letter into my hand. "Hide this. We can't let them find it. I'll try to slow them down." She staggered downstairs. Xiao Hong-yin hurried out behind her.

I stood there dumbly. Searches were not allowed now without permission of the police. How could they be searching us? We had already been searched once before.

The loud voices on the stairs shook me awake. I looked at the letter—the thick, heavy letter that Mom and Uncle Tian had written to the Municipal Party Committee. My hand began to shake.

I rushed into the room and looked around desperately. No, the room would be thoroughly ransacked. I ran back out to the kitchen. Behind the sink? No. I dashed into the bathroom. Toilet tank? No. Where? Where should I hide it? I could not think. I could feel the blood throbbing in my temples.

Suddenly I remembered Little White's litter box. I dashed up to the roof. By the time I had smoothed out the ashes and walked downstairs, the searchers were already at the door.

Mom stood in the doorway, trying to keep Thin-Face from rushing in. "The Municipal Party Committee has directed that no searches are allowed without permission of the police."

Thin-Face sneered. He fished a piece of paper out of his pocket and thrust it in front of Mom's nose. "Read this. The authorities have determined that Jiang

Xi-reng is a landlord who has escaped detection and gone unpunished. You're a damned landlord's wife." He threw the paper in Mom's face and rushed into the room with his crew.

What a ransacking!

They had brought big lights and thick wires from the theater and strung them through the room and on the roof and balcony. The whole apartment blazed like a movie set. We could hear the hubbub from the crowd of spectators outside in the alley.

Thin-Face and his crew were methodical and thorough. They emptied every trunk and every drawer, tore the beds and sofa apart, and even searched the dusty attic carefully.

One woman found the rags cut from Grandma's old gowns. "We can piece these together and use them for the Landlord Jiang Xi-reng's struggle meeting. It is excellent proof of his luxurious lifestyle," she said excitedly, and the whole box was carried away. Someone else saw the round porcelain stool under the window. It was cracked, so we had not been able to sell it like the other one. "This is a valuable antique from the Qian-long period," he said. The stool was taken away.

★ ★ ★

The search went on and on. Ji-yun, Ji-yong, and I sat in a corner of the room, trembling at the slamming of the wardrobe and the chests. My mind was entirely on the letter under the ashes. Suddenly Ji-yong stood up and walked toward one of the ransackers.

"I borrowed that book." He pointed toward a pile that the man was going to carry away.

"What? What did you say?" The young man turned around and arrogantly looked down on Ji-yong.

"I borrowed that book. I need to return it."

The young man pulled the book out of the pile. *"The Wild Animals I Have Raised,"* he read aloud. He scrutinized the book and then looked back at Ji-yong.

"Do you know what kind of book this is?"

"No. What kind is it?"

"It's a translation that propagates the bourgeois theory of humanitarism."

"I don't care what it propagates. I borrowed it and I have to return it tomorrow." Ji-yong was feeling obstinate.

"You've got some nerve for a little black bastard. How dare you plead for this damned revisionist book?" He held the book in front of Ji-yong's face and very slowly began tearing the cover off.

Ji-yong rushed toward him and tried to grab the

book. The man grabbed Ji-yong's collar and pulled my brother toward him, and then suddenly pushed away. Ji-yong staggered several steps backward and fell on a heap of clothes. He tried to stand up and rush at the man again, but Ji-yun and I jumped on him and held him down.

"He hit me! Let me go! Let me go!" His eyes were filled with tears. He struggled violently under our arms. I could feel his gasps against my face.

While we were struggling to hold Ji-yong down, Six-Fingers bustled in. He pulled Thin-Face into a corner and whispered something, then left.

Thin-Face watched us struggling like a hunter watching the animals in his trap. Ji-yong stopped fighting, and I straightened up.

"We've seen a lot of each other lately, haven't we?" He gave a grimace meant to suggest a smile. "According to reliable sources, you hid a very important letter just before we arrived." He paused and examined our reactions carefully. "Here is the opportunity for you to help Chairman Mao's revolution. Who can win the most honor by telling us first?"

I felt an intense rush of heat, as if my whole body were flushed.

"This was reported by a member of the revolutionary

masses." He was talking only to me now. "We even know where it was hidden, but before I go get it, I'll give you one last chance to prove your loyalty to Chairman Mao. And then . . ."

It must have been Ji-yun's classmate Xiao Hong-yin, I thought. She was there when Mom gave me the letter. She must have reported it. But she didn't see me hide the letter. They couldn't know where it was.

Seeing that there was no response, Thin-Face took off his smiling mask. He stepped in front of me, bent over, and suddenly shouted in my face, "Don't you know, or is it just that you don't want to talk?"

I shivered. Ji-yun grasped my shirt and buried her face in my back. Thin-Face's head was only inches from mine. His bloodshot eyes bulged out so much that the whites seemed much larger than usual. His skin was red with rage. He looked so savage that I shrank back, sure that he was going to hit me. I shut my eyes and clenched my teeth. "I don't know."

My heart pounded. I waited. Nothing happened. I opened my eyes.

"So you don't want to talk," he snarled. "I think I can figure out a way to help you." He straightened up and shouted to the young man who had torn the book. "Bring the two landlords' wives in here!"

Grandma was leaning heavily on Mom as they came into the room.

Thin-Face was in front of them immediately. "Leniency for those who confess, severity for those who resist. I'm sure you remember that. Now. Where did you hide the letter? Confess!"

Mom's face changed color. Grandma looked at him and replied timidly, "Letter? What letter?"

"Damn you!" Thin-Face slapped her face with all his strength. Grandma staggered into Mom's arms.

"Grandma!" We all sprang to our feet and rushed to Grandma.

"She's over seventy, you— How could you?" Shielding Grandma with her own body, Mom shouted back at Thin-Face.

"Over seventy! So what? Damned old landlord's wife!" Thin-Face held his hand. He must have hurt it when he slapped Grandma. "Old landlord's wife, kneel down and face the wall. Stay there until you confess. You—" He turned to the rest of us. "You all sit here and watch. Don't go near her. If you care about her, confess. Otherwise she'll stay there forever. We'll see who's stronger." He walked out.

Grandma knelt down facing the wall. I could see the red marks of Thin-Face's fingers on her face. Her whole body was trembling so violently that I could see her linen shirt shaking.

"Grandma . . ." Ji-yun cried out suddenly. Tears were rolling down my cheeks too.

"Don't you cry for her. She's an exploiting landlord's wife." The young man stepped up to Ji-yun. "If you keep crying, I'll make your mother kneel down too."

I looked at Mom. Her face was terribly haggard. She looked as if she were about to faint. She took out her handkerchief and wiped Ji-yun's face. "Don't cry, dear, don't cry. Everything will be all right," she said softly.

Grandma was sitting limply on her legs now, supporting her weight on her hands just like Old Qian had that day. A few white hairs clung to her red cheek.

Maybe I should tell, I thought frantically. Grandma was so frail. . . . But then would we all get into bigger trouble? What should I do? What should I do, Mom? I stole several glances at Mom, but she hung her head and stared at the ground.

After a long while the young man went into the bathroom. No one else was watching us. Mom whispered in my ear, "Where's the letter?"

"In Little White's litter box. Are you going to tell them?"

Mom shook her head hesitantly. She looked at Grandma and murmured, "I'm afraid she can't stand any more. It looks like they won't give up till they find it."

We were interrupted by a hubbub. Heavy footsteps rushed up to the roof. For a few minutes there was silence. Then suddenly we heard a crowd of people pounding down the stairs, roaring with coarse laughter.

"The cat did a great job. We should give her a reward."

"But the letter stinks of cat piss."

The letter!

I sagged weakly to the chair. Little White must have revealed the letter by raking up the ashes after she had used her box.

Thin-Face dashed into the room, his face lit with a sinister smile of victory. "What did I say? Who won? Who was stronger, you or the iron fist of the Proletarian Dictatorship? Humph!" He waved the letter in Mom's face. "So you thought you could reverse the verdict, did you? Hah!" he grunted in satisfaction. "Chen Ying, tomorrow you will report to your work unit that you are a landlord's wife now. We will inform them of what happened today, and will invite you as a companion to your husband's struggle meeting."

He stood over Grandma, who was still on the floor. "Old landlord's wife, starting tomorrow you will sweep the alley like the other landlords' wives. You have been lucky that we didn't expose you earlier. Go register at the Neighborhood Dictatorship Group at eight."

He turned and was about to walk out when he saw me.

"You," he snorted. Even in his elation his eyes froze me. "You have just missed your opportunity to be an educable child. Too bad. We will let your school know all about your firm class stance."

It was now four thirty in the morning. The alley was deserted. The huge truck, loaded with most of our possessions, blew its horn in the deadly silence and triumphantly left.

The dark world became quiet, as quiet as the inside of a grave.

We gathered around Mom and Grandma. Song Po-po tiptoed up from her room and joined us. The furniture was gone, and most of our possessions, but at the moment we could not worry about that. The letter, the letter we had worried about all night, was gone. That was all we could think about.

"We have to tell Uncle Tian about the letter right away. He'll be in trouble as soon as he gets to work."

Mom's voice sounded horrifying in the silence.

"I wonder if the guards at the entrance to the alley are gone yet. They won't let us go if they're still there," Grandma said weakly.

"We have to try. There's no other way."

Song Po-po spoke up softly. "I can go take a look. I'll just go out as if I'm buying soy milk. No one will notice."

"You're not afraid?" Mom asked.

"No."

Grandma patted Song Po-po's hand gratefully. There was nothing we could say.

She left with a small pot for soy milk, looking weak and tired.

In less than five minutes she hurried back. "Mrs. Jiang, they're still there. You can't go."

"What can we do now?" Grandma was anxious. "It will be too late soon."

"I can go." In surprise we turned toward Ji-yong, who had been silent until now. "I can climb over the back wall. I've done it lots of times with my friends," he added when he saw our doubtful looks.

Mom had no other choice.

"When you get there, remember not to ring the bell or call his name loudly. Just go to the back of the house and knock softly at the bedroom window. Don't let anyone hear you!" She repeated her directions over and over as she gave him the bus fare.

We watched him dissolve into the misty dawn.

Everyone was exhausted. Mom helped Grandma lie down on a pile of clothes, and the rest of us just sank down where we were. We lay in the grayish darkness, silent but awake, listening for Ji-yong's footsteps.

A century passed. The sky was brightening when we finally heard creaking on the stairs. We all sat up, looking at him hopefully. His listless face told us everything.

"I knocked at all the windows for a long time, but nobody answered. Maybe they already came and took him away."

Mom let out a despairing sigh and buried her face in her hands. Grandma lay down again and moaned softly. Ji-yong, Ji-yun, and I sat looking at each other, with no idea what we should do.

The sun had risen as usual, but nothing else about the day was the same as the day before.

Ji-yong went with Mom to report to her work unit that she had now been classified as a landlord's wife. Ji-yun and I were to accompany Grandma to the Neighborhood Dictatorship Group to register.

Before we left, I stood in the doorway and gazed at the remains of our home. The mahogany furniture was gone. The four repainted trunks were gone. So was the sofa. We had no beds, no table, no chairs—only an old-fashioned desk lying on its side in one corner and a jumbled pile of clothes in the middle of the floor.

My body was an empty shell, too devastated to feel anything but exhaustion. I could not fight anymore. As I trembled down the stairs with Grandma, a thought came to me for the first time in my life.

Should I continue to live at all?

SWEEPING

Kneeling on the broken bamboo stool under the window, I peeked anxiously through the curtains.

It had rained yesterday, a cold, day-long autumn rain. The leaves and scraps of paper were stuck to the pavement of the alley. Grandma was sweeping slowly and carefully. She held the long broom handle tightly against her, and her whole body swayed back and forth as she struggled to clean the pavement.

I wished that she could sweep faster. Although every single neighbor and classmate knew what had happened to my family, I could not bear to have them see Grandma sweeping.

I heard a moan and turned around. Mom was lying on the straw mat on the floor behind me. Her face was colorless and hollow. Her temples were gray. Yesterday she had fainted again.

A few weeks after the ransack, I could still hardly recognize our home. It had become a barren warehouse.

Our beds were straw mats on the floor. Our few clothes were in a packing crate Ji-yong had found on the street. Our table was the lid of a crate laid across two benches.

I turned back to the alley. Grandma leaned stiffly over to scrape up a stubborn piece of newspaper that would not come off with the broom. I winced as I watched her bend her swollen knees and slowly straighten up again.

Life was very hard, so hard that I could hardly breathe sometimes. I not only needed to manage our limited income and take care of Mom's bad health, I had to bear the stares and the gossiping of our neighbors and attend the study sessions at school. But these were not my biggest worries. The worry of tomorrow haunted me constantly. I worried that Grandma would be sent to the countryside, as other landlords had been, and would be punished by the farmers there. I worried that Mom would be detained for attempting to help Dad. I worried that Dad would be beaten to death for his stubbornness. I worried that Ji-yong's temper would get him in trouble, and that Ji-yun would be so frightened that she would never laugh again. Worst of all, I worried that by not hiding the letter well enough, I had ruined our lives forever.

Sometimes I had thought of running away, joining

a student reeducation troop in a distant province.

Sometimes I had thought I did not want to live.

It was Mom who had stopped me.

Five days after the ransack, Mom was still very sick. I was helping her wash her hair.

"Ji-li," Mom said suddenly. "If anything happens to your Grandma and me, remember, you're the oldest. Make sure you take good care of your brother and sister."

I felt tears in my eyes. "Mom, what are you talking about?"

Mom sat up straight and opened her eyes. "You know our situation. Anything can happen." She paused before she said, "Maybe we should let my sister adopt Ji-yun. Your aunt's family has no bad connections. Maybe Ji-yun would be better off—"

"No!" The cry jerked out before I knew it. "Mom, don't. Please. I will take care of both of them. I promise."

As soon as I said it, I realized that I had made my promise to them—to everyone in my family—long ago. I had promised during the days that Grandma and I had hidden in the park; I had promised when I had not testified against Dad; I had promised when I had hidden the letter. I would never do anything to hurt my family, and I would do everything I could to take care of them.

My family was too precious to forget, and too rare to replace.

Grandma lifted her head and stretched her back. I ducked behind the curtain so that she wouldn't see me. Every day I watched until she was finished. When I was seven, Grandma watched and waited for me at this very window when I walked back from school every afternoon. Now it was my turn to watch her and take care of her. I no longer worried that she was a landlord's wife. She was my grandmother.

Once my life had been defined by my goals: to be a *da-dui-zhang,* to participate in the exhibition, to be a Red Guard. They seemed unimportant to me now. Now my life was defined by my responsibilities. I had promised to take care of my family, and I would renew that promise every day. I could not give up or withdraw, no matter how hard life became. I would hide my tears and my fear for Mom and Grandma's sake. It was my turn to take care of them.

The clouds dispersed and the sky lightened a bit. Grandma picked up her broom and turned stiffly around to come home.

"Another day." I took a deep breath and shook my head. "I will do my job. I will."

EPILOGUE

Many friends have asked me why, after all I went through, I did not hate Chairman Mao and the Cultural Revolution in those years. The answer is simple: We were all brainwashed.

To us Chairman Mao was God. He controlled everything we read, everything we heard, and everything we learned in school. We believed everything he said. Naturally, we knew only good things about Chairman Mao and the Cultural Revolution. Anything bad had to be the fault of others. Mao was blameless.

When I started to write this book, I asked An Yi's mother if she had hated Mao when she was forced to climb the factory chimney. "I didn't hate him," she told me. "I believed that the Cultural Revolution was necessary to prevent revisionism and capitalism from taking over China. I knew that I was wronged, but mistakes happen under any system. If the country was better for the movement that persecuted me, I was still in favor of it. It was only after Mao's death that I knew I was deceived."

It *was* only after Mao's death in 1976 that people woke up. We finally learned that the whole Cultural Revolution had been part of a power struggle at the highest levels of the Party. Our leader had taken advantage of our trust and loyalty to manipulate the whole country. This is the most frightening lesson of the Cultural Revolution: Without a sound legal system, a small group or even a single person can take control of an entire country. This is as true now as it was then.

Thirty years have passed since I was the little girl with the red scarf who believed she would always succeed at everything. I grew up and moved to the United States, but still, whatever I did, wherever I went, vivid memories of my childhood kept coming back to me. After thinking so much about that time, I wanted to do something for the little girl I had been, and for all the children who lost their childhoods as I did. This book is the result.

This book tells of my experiences between the ages of twelve and fourteen. I have presented my family as it was, but in order to protect the privacy of friends and neighbors mentioned in the story, I have changed their names and some details of their stories.

And what happened since then?

A few months after our ransack the revolutionary situation in the theater changed again. The Rebels who had taken control lost power to a new group. Most of those who had been detained were released, including Uncle Fan, Aunt Wu, and Uncle Tian, who was detained right after our ransack because of the letter. Dad finally returned home too. He was still considered a landlord, and was put to work as a janitor; Mom still had to write self-criticism reports because she would not break with Dad; and Grandma still had to sweep the alley twice a day, but at least we were all together again.

Our class status continued to hold us back. Because of our political background I was denied another opportunity to become a stage actress, just as Ji-yong was not allowed to become a trumpeter nor Ji-yun a singer. But we never gave up. When the schools reopened after the Cultural Revolution, we all went to universities to finish our education. Both Ji-yun and I became teachers, while Ji-yong worked in a watch factory.

In 1980 my father was finally cleared. Not only was the charge that he was an "escaped landlord" dropped, but an old decision made during the Antirightist Movement was reversed as well. Only then did I learn the whole story. As a university student Dad had risked his life by joining the Communist Party when it was still an illegal, underground organization. During the Antirightist Movement of 1958, Dad had expressed some disagreement with Party policies, and as a result he was forced to resign from the Party. Although he was never officially classified as a rightist, he was denied promotions and major roles, and his career was ruined. In 1980 he was "rehabilitated" and appointed Vice President of the Children's Art Theater. I looked at his gray hair and felt sad rather than happy. I knew he loved acting more than anything, and knew that nothing could make up for all the years he had lost.

The years of disappointments finally made me move to the United States. Now the whole family is here, except for Grandma, who died in 1992 at the age of ninety-eight. Ji-yong lives in Seattle, where he works in the tourist industry. Ji-yun teaches in a community college nearby, and my parents live with her family and enjoy the company of their two grandsons. And at long last my father has been able to do some acting.

Song Po-po died of a stroke not long after I came to America.

Sometimes when I think of all we went through, I can't help feeling that it was only by the grace of God that we were saved. My parents and Grandma all admitted that at times during those dark years they contemplated suicide. Without God's blessing they could never have survived.

As for the others in my story, in the early 1970s nearly all of my contemporaries were sent to the countryside for "reeducation." According to Mao, this was supposed to benefit both the young students and the farmers. The students would learn to respect the working masses, and the farmers would learn new technology from the students. Like the Cultural Revolution, this did not work out as it was supposed to. After ten years of sacrifice in the primitive countryside most of these young people returned to the city with little education, few skills, and no beliefs. All regretted the waste of their youth, and all have struggled to start over again.

Chang Hong worked for many years on a state-run farm near Mongolia. Her brother died while she was there. At the farm she met her husband. Ironically, he was a black whelp, the son of a former capitalist. Eventually they returned to Shanghai, where Chang Hong was able to move into a factory job.

An Yi's asthma prevented her from being sent to the

countryside, and all these years she has been working in a small factory. Bai Shan spent years in the remote countryside near the Russian border, but now he is the business manager of the Shanghai branch of a foreign company. Lin-lin went back to school and became a doctor at a factory clinic. In the recent economic upheavals her factory closed, and the last time I saw her she was still unemployed. Du Hai is working in a factory near our childhood homes, and I saw him once at a distance. I've never heard what happened to Yin Lan-lan.

Except for a few who actually killed people, hardly any "revolutionaries" have been punished for what they did during the Cultural Revolution. Those who persecuted others, even beat or tortured them, were victims too, after all. They all believed they were doing it for Chairman Mao. In fact, many were caught on the wrong side in the power struggles and were persecuted in their turn, just as Du Hai's mother was.

I once fervently believed in Mao and the Chinese Communist Party. After all the experiences I have told about in this story, and many more painful and frustrating experiences afterward, I left China and moved to the United States in 1984. I was thirty years old. I started at the bottom. I had no money, no friends, and hardly any English. I was willing to take on the struggle to establish myself in a new country because I knew that was the price I would have to pay for the freedom to think, speak, and write whatever I pleased.

During my first few years in the United States I was continually astonished at the freedom Americans enjoy. One Halloween evening I was watching the parade at Waikiki Beach in Honolulu. I was amazed to see that all the celebrators were enjoying themselves so freely. They had no fear of being criticized by their bosses or arrested by the government for expressing themselves, even if they criticized or mocked the president.

After my graduation from the University of Hawaii in 1987 I worked for a hotel and resort chain for several years, then for a health care company. Despite my success and promotions, I was not entirely happy. I realized that although I have adopted a new country, I cannot forget China. I wonder about China's present, and I worry about her future. I have realized that despite all my suffering, I cannot stop loving the country where I was born and raised. Feeling as I do, it seemed natural for me to start my own company, East West Exchange, to promote cultural exchanges between the United States and China. If I can help Americans to understand China, and the Chinese to learn about the United

States, even a little, I will feel very rewarded. I will have contributed something to my country, China, and my home, America.

I hope this book will be part of that mission.

acupuncture: An ancient Chinese medical practice, in which very thin needles are inserted into specific points in the skin in order to relieve a wide variety of ailments. Acupuncture is often used to relieve the pain of arthritis, headaches, etc.

Allah: The Moslem name for God. Moslems are a religious minority in China. Most Chinese Moslems live in western China, but there are some, like the Jiang family, who live in eastern cities such as Shanghai.

Beijing: The capital of China. Formerly spelled "Peking."

black: Opposed to the Communist Party. Communism was symbolized by the color red. Black, seen as the opposite of red, was used to symbolize opponents of Communism, and therefore became a negative in general.

black whelp: An insulting term for a child of a family belonging to any one of the "Five Black Categories."

bourgeois; bourgeoisie: A member of the middle class. In China this term is used in a derogatory manner to describe a person who enjoys and admires a luxurious "capitalist" lifestyle.

capitalism: An economic system characterized by private ownership of property, free competition, and business for profit. The United States, Japan, and many other countries are capitalist nations. Communists are strongly opposed to capitalism. (See "Communism.")

Central Committee: The powerful top leadership of the Chinese Communist Party, which actually rules the country. They make laws, issue policies, and control the military, legal systems, and even the national treasury. Chairman Mao was the head of the Central Committee.

Chairman Mao: See "Mao Ze-dong."

Chiang Kai-shek (1887–1975): The chairman of the Nationalist Party, and one of Mao Ze-dong's major enemies. Before 1949 he was the leader of China. In 1949 he was defeated by Mao Ze-dong and the Communist Party and fled to the offshore island of Taiwan, where he continued as the chairman of the Nationalist Party until his death.

Chinese New Year: The most important family holiday in China. Chinese New Year is the first day of the lunar calendar, which is based on the phases of the moon. The date varies according to the Western calendar, but Chinese New Year usually occurs in late January or early February.

class status: A system of classifying people by their economic situation or occupation. This was particularly important during the Cultural Revolution. It was believed that family class status would determine one's behavior and thinking, so someone born in a family with a "red" class status was assumed to be revolutionary, while one born into a "black" family was assumed to be unreliable. One's status was determined by one's father's degree of "redness" or "blackness."

Communism: An economic system in which all means of production, such as land and natural resources, are owned by the entire community and used for the good of all its members.

Communist Party: China's ruling political party, led during his lifetime by Chairman Mao.

conservative: One who resists political change. To Chinese Communists the term was usually negative, but during the Cultural Revolution the meaning could change. Sometimes the people called conservatives were more loyal to the Communist leadership than the so-called revolutionaries.

counterrevolutionary: A person who actively fights against the Communist Party. A counterrevolutionary is seen as a public enemy.

crematorium: The building where the bodies of the dead are cremated—that is, burned. Nonreligious memorial services were performed at the crematorium, since all religion was condemned as superstition during the Cultural Revolution. In China today bodies are usually cremated, because land is considered too valuable to use for graves.

criticize: In China during the Cultural Revolution criticizing was punishment for political errors. "Criticism" was often carried out in "struggle meetings" and often included humiliation or physical punishment.

Cultural Revolution (officially known as the Great Proletarian Cultural Revolution): The social and political upheaval that overtook China from 1966 to 1976. During this time many innocent people were ruthlessly persecuted. The Cultural Revolution was launched by Chairman Mao, supposedly to rid the country of anti-Communist influences. Long afterward it was revealed that Chairman Mao unleashed this chaos in order to protect his own political position.

da-dui-zhang: In a Chinese elementary school, the student chairman of the entire school, roughly equivalent to the Student Council president in an American school.

da-zi-bao: A form of propaganda in the shape of a large handwritten poster presenting an important issue. During the Cultural Revolution, *da-zi-bao* were used to attack and humiliate people.

detainment: Confinement without legal arrest. People who were under investigation were often put in solitary confinement within their work units as a way to make them confess, sometimes falsely, to political crimes.

educable child: In Cultural Revolution jargon, a child from a "black" family who is loyal to the Communist Party and rejects his or her black family.

establish revolutionary ties: In Cultural Revolution jargon, to meet with people from other regions to exchange the experience of the Cultural Revolution and discuss political issues.

exploitation: The unethical use of someone else's labor or resources for one's own profit.

fen: The Chinese "penny," one hundredth of a yuan.

feudalism: The economic system in which the majority of the land was held by relatively few landowners, who leased their vast properties to farmers in return for large shares of the crops.

Five Black Categories: According to Chairman Mao and the Communist Party, the worst enemies of Communism and the common people. The five categories were: landlords, rich peasants, counterrevolutionaries, criminals, and rightists.

Four Olds: "Old ideas, old culture, old customs, and old habits." According to the propaganda, these remnants of the old society interfered with the creation of a modern, socialist society. However, people in power arbitrarily decided whether or not something was "fourolds," and used this as an excuse to attack people and destroy property.

ideology: A system of beliefs. Communist theory held that in order to change social conditions, people needed to change their patterns of thought. Someone with "bad ideology" was dragging the society backward, so this was a serious matter. The Cultural Revolution's emphasis on changing "old thinking" made ideology even more important.

individualist: One who believes that each individual is more important than the group as a whole, and who favors freedom of action and belief. Individualism was in opposition to the Communist theory of the supremacy of the state, and therefore it was considered a moral weakness.

Lao Jiang: "Lao" literally means "old." It is a common way to address friends or acquaintances who are older than the speaker.

Lei Feng (1940–1962): A soldier in the People's Liberation Army who was noted for his good deeds. He was held up as a model for ordinary people to emulate.

Liberation: The establishment of the Chinese Communist government in 1949 by Chairman Mao; so called because the Communist Party claimed to be liberating the common people from feudalism and from Chiang Kai-shek's oppression.

Liu Shao-qi (1898–1974): The chairman of the nation (or head of state) and vice-chairman of the Communist

Party when the Cultural Revolution started. He was second in command to Mao, who was the chairman of the Communist Party. In China the Communist Party always has the highest power over the nation, the military force, and so on. Mao was threatened by the power Liu and other leaders were gaining, and launched the Cultural Revolution to suppress them. Liu was overthrown at the end of 1966, and later was placed under house arrest for a few years before he died. Also spelled "Liu Shao-chi."

Mandarin: The official national language of China. The many regions of China have their own local languages; the Chinese are encouraged to speak Mandarin so that people from different areas can communicate with each other.

Mao Ze-dong (1893–1976): The chairman of the Chinese Communist Party, and leader of China from 1949 to 1976. Formerly spelled Mao Tse-tung.

Mao Ze-dong Thought Study Groups: Groups that gathered at schools, workplaces, or neighborhoods to study Chairman Mao's works. The Communist Party encouraged these groups as a way to educate people and strengthen the power of the Party.

Nanjing: A city on the Yangtze River about 200 miles from Shanghai. Formerly spelled "Nanking."

Nationalist Party: The party of Chiang Kai-shek,

which ruled China from 1928 until the Communist victory in 1949. The Nationalist Party led a revolution against the emperor in 1911 and tried to establish a democracy. They were defeated by the Communist Party in 1949 and withdrew to Taiwan. The Nationalists continue to rule the island of Taiwan today.

Neighborhood Dictatorship Groups: During the Cultural Revolution, volunteer groups that monitored the activities of neighbors. Since they were not official organizations, their duties and formats varied from city to city.

Neighborhood Party Committee: The Communist Party officers in charge of a neighborhood.

neutral: In Communist jargon, neither "red" nor "black." Since anything neutral was not sufficiently "red," to be neutral meant to be weak.

office workers: The class that was neither "black" nor "red." "Office workers" included intellectuals and professionals, salespeople, and people who worked in offices. They were not considered as admirable as farmers or factory workers.

pedicab: A three-wheeled vehicle pedaled like a bicycle, with a seat for one or two passengers behind the driver. Sometimes called a bicycle rickshaw.

People's Liberation Army: The national army of Communist China.

political study class: A gathering in a neighborhood, workplace, or school to study Mao's writings or the Communist Party's documents. For people who were said to have political mistakes, these classes were often used to pressure them into confessing their problems.

Precious Red Book: The common name for a pocket-sized edition of *Selected Quotations from the Writings of Chairman Mao*. During the Cultural Revolution it was quoted frequently in schools, workplaces, and political meetings. Many people, especially Red Guards and enthusiastic revolutionaries, carried it everywhere.

proletarian: A member of the working class, especially a farmer or factory worker.

propaganda: Information intended to promote a particular belief. While sometimes the word implies that the information is false, or at least misleading, in Communist China it was used as a positive term, something like "public relations."

reactionary: Against the Communist Revolution, or a person who is against the revolution.

Rebel: Someone fighting for political change. To Chinese Communists this was generally considered a positive term during the Cultural Revolution.

red: The symbolic color of Communism. Therefore, any person who conforms to Communist Party ideology is considered "red," as is anything that serves to further the cause of Communism.

Red Guard: During the Cultural Revolution a very popular, semiformal organization of high school and college students who were from "red" family backgrounds or who, though not "red," had proved themselves to be firm revolutionaries. They were Chairman Mao's loyal supporters and the pioneers of the Cultural Revolution.

Red Successors: A semiformal organization in elementary schools formed in imitation of the Red Guards.

reeducation troop: A group of students from the city who were sent (or volunteered to go) to the remote countryside to work with the farmers as part of their education.

reincarnation: The belief, held by China's majority Buddhists among others, that after death a soul is reborn in another body.

remold one's ideology: In Communist jargon, improve or correct one's beliefs. For people who had made important political mistakes, this meant they were expected to change or correct their beliefs to match those of the Central Committee.

revisionist: A member of the Communist Party who attempts to alter Communist ideals. This was a very serious offense during the Cultural Revolution.

Revolutionary Committee: A group in charge of any

organization or company within China. This term was invented by the Central Committee during the Cultural Revolution to replace the former leadership. Revolutionary Committees were formed in every unit: schools, factories, farms, the armed services, etc.

Revolutionary Performance Team: An informal student group that promoted Communist ideals. Formed by school revolutionary committees, or by the students themselves, these groups performed songs and skits in schools, and sometimes for the public.

rightist: A member of a conservative party who disagreed with or opposed the Communist Party.

sanitary belt: A washable and reusable cotton pad used during menstruation.

school committee: A central group appointed by the Communist Party to be in charge of school administration.

Shanghai: China's largest city. During the Cultural Revolution it had a population of about 10 million people.

socialism: An economic system in which government ownership of land, industries, transport, natural resources, and so on, is supposed to help distribute wealth more evenly between the rich and the poor.

struggle meeting: A meeting within a work unit to publicly criticize someone. Often these meetings included humiliation or even physical assault. This format was not officially ordered by the Central Committee, but it was used as an effective revolutionary weapon.

study group: A nonofficial small group that gathered regularly to study a particular subject, often a political issue, such as Chairman Mao's works or Lei Feng's Diary.

study session: A small meeting intended to change someone's behavior or thinking by studying Mao's works and government documents. Held as needed, these sessions were used to improve revolutionaries and reeducate others.

summer labor: Under the Communist government, a regular part of education, in which students take part in factory or farm work during school vacations in order to learn to appreciate the contribution of the laboring masses.

telephone kiosk: Before private telephones were common, a small booth containing one or two phones served an entire community. Usually two people who worked in the kiosk would take and deliver messages.

work unit: The term for any organization that employs a person.

Uncle; Aunt: Polite titles used by children when addressing adults, especially family friends.

xenophile: A person who loves anything foreign. Such behavior was considered disloyal.

yin-yang hairdo: A punishment in which one side of the head is shaved and the hair is left long on the other.

Young Pioneers: A primary-school group that included most children in every school. Approved by the school committee, membership in the Young Pioneers was intended as the first step toward eventual membership in the Communist Party.

yuan: The Chinese "dollar." During the Cultural Revolution the official value of a yuan was about one third of a U.S. dollar.